Avoiding Auto Repair Rip-offs

Avoiding Auto Repair Rip-offs

Arthur P. Glickman and the Editors of Consumer Reports Books

Consumer Reports Books
A Division of Consumers Union
Yonkers, New York

The editors of Consumer Reports Books would like to thank
Alex Markovich for his invaluable assistance.

Copyright © 1995 by Arthur P. Glickman and
Consumers Union of United States, Inc., Yonkers, New York 10703.

Published by Consumers Union of United States, Inc., Yonkers, New York 10703.

Library of Congress Cataloging-in-Publication Data

Avoiding auto repair rip-offs / Arthur P. Glickman and the
   editors of Consumer Reports Books.
       p.   cm.
    Includes index.
    ISBN 0-89043-761-0
    1. Automobiles—Maintenance and repair—United States.
2. Automobile industry and trade—United States. 3. Consumer
education—United States. I. Glickman, Arthur P. II. Consumer
Reports Books.
TL152.H8452   1995
629.28'72'0296—dc20   94-24961
                                           CIP

Design by Joseph Dephino

First printing, May 1995

This book is printed on recycled paper.

Manufactured in the United States of America

Avoiding Auto Repair Rip-offs is a Consumer Reports Book published by Consumers Union, the
nonprofit organization that publishes *Consumer Reports*, the monthly magazine of test reports,
product Ratings, and buying guidance. Established in 1936, Consumers Union is chartered under
the Not-for-Profit Corporation Law of the State of New York.
    The purposes of Consumers Union, as stated in its charter, are to provide consumers with
information and counsel on consumer goods and services, to give information on all matters relating
to the expenditure of the family income, and to initiate and to cooperate with individual and group
efforts seeking to create and maintain decent living standards.
    Consumers Union derives its income solely from the sale of *Consumer Reports* and other
publications. In addition, expenses of occasional public service efforts may be met, in part, by
nonrestrictive, noncommercial contributions, grants, and fees. Consumers Union accepts no
advertising or product samples and is not beholden in any way to any commercial interest. Its
Ratings and reports are solely for the use of the readers of its publications. Neither the Ratings, nor
the reports, nor any Consumers Union publications, including this book, may be used in advertising
or for any commercial purpose. Consumers Union will take all steps open to it to prevent such uses
of its material, its name, or the name of *Consumer Reports*.

To my niece, Debra Lynn Smith

Contents

PART TWO
What to Do if You've Been Hornswoggled

PART THREE
Consumer Reports Survey

Avoiding Auto Repair Rip-offs

Introduction

"I would rather go to the dentist without Novocain than to an auto repair shop," says talk show host Phil Donahue.

Apparently most people agree.

When the American Use of Time Project at the University of Maryland asked 2,500 adults to rate about 200 ordinary activities, going to an auto repair shop was the most disliked activity —just beating out a visit to the dentist.

The biggest fear of those who seek car repairs is that the job will be bungled—that cars will not be repaired right the first, second, or even third time in the shop.

Being taken advantage of because one lacks technical knowledge about cars is another common concern. All too many mechanics, it seems, are ready to cheat those who might think a MacPherson strut is some sort of Scottish folk dance.

The high level of bungling and banditry is reflected in a 1994 survey of consumer protection agencies by the Consumer Federation of America. It found that auto repairs generated the third most complaints, behind dissatisfaction with new- and used-car purchases (we'll get to them in a moment) and home improvement. In all, 55 percent of the agencies responding to the survey ranked auto repairs among their top five complaints.

Surveys over the past several decades tend to validate most people's fears that the giant sucking sound one hears at many auto repair shops is one's wallet being lifted. Most such surveys indicate that, *at best*, you probably have a fifty-fifty chance of going into an auto repair shop at random and getting your car repaired correctly and without being cheated.

Here are a few of these investigations:

1. In 1993 a reporter from *Ladies' Home Journal* took a 1990 Dodge Spirit to six garages at random in New Jersey, New York, and Connecticut. Either the car had a partially unplugged fuel injector wire (causing the Dodge to misfire and idle roughly, and making the Check Engine light come on) or it had a nonworking headlight resulting from a blown fuse.

   Two of the three mechanics who worked on the injector wire cheated the woman driver. The first shop charged $176.49 for new spark plugs, ignition wires, distributor cap, and rotor (labor was extra). In addition, the mechanic caused the car to run badly. He had broken the center electrode on the new distributor cap, hadn't fastened the air cleaner down, and installed a cracked spark plug wire.

   The second garage charged $95.33 for computer diagnostic time and new spark plugs, which weren't installed. The third facility found and fixed the problem, charging $31.16 for diagnostic time.

   The headlight repair turned out better. Only one of three mechanics cheated the driver. That mechanic replaced the $2 fuse but charged $26.50 for a new headlight.

2. In Las Vegas, KTNV-TV found in 1993 that their chances were probably better at the city's blackjack tables than at local auto repair shops. Reporters selected 10 repair shops at random and felt they got a fair deal from only two of them.

    They used two different cars: a 1988 Chevrolet Beretta with a hole ripped in the vacuum hose that attached to an engine sensor and a 1989 Toyota Camry with a set of transmission wires disconnected, which caused the car to stick in third gear.

    For the Chevy's problem—normally a $20 to $50 repair—one shop did a four-hour diagnostic test running $130 and then recommended $200 in repairs. For the Camry, one shop didn't bother to reconnect the wires, but it charged $790 to rebuild the transmission.
3. In 1992, the New Jersey Division of Consumer Affairs took a car with a disconnected alternator wire to 38 repair shops—on two separate occasions. Sixty percent of the shops did an incorrect diagnosis or recommended unnecessary repairs.

(To be fair, at least one recent investigation found repair shops to be quite honest. In 1991, WCBD-TV in Charleston, South Carolina, took a car with an induced vacuum hose problem to 52 local repair shops. Only one shop tried to rip off the young woman driver, who portrayed herself as a damsel in distress. In Pennsylvania, *only* 7 of some 35 shops visited by the state attorney general's office in 1989 sold or tried to sell unneeded repairs.)

Nevertheless, some members of the auto repair business are so corrupt that, during a 1988 investigation, the *Record* of Hackensack, New Jersey, found many instances of lying among mechanics who considered themselves honest. A mechanic who rated his shop's honesty at 9.5 on a scale of 10 charged $55.30 for a new oil pressure switch and repairing a wire behind the fuse box—work that was never done. He said he had spent 1½ hours working on the car before realizing a fuse was causing the problem. Another mechanic, who urged the newspaper to investigate a chain store for wanting to do $300 worth of unneeded work on the car on his lift, himself charged $15.90 for a minor alignment adjustment that he didn't do. His partner charged $8.48 for fixing some wires he said were rubbing together, when in fact he merely replaced a burned-out fuse.

The true cost of auto repair rip-offs is difficult to quantify. The last scientific study was done in the mid-1970s. At that time, a federally sponsored diagnostic center operating in Huntsville, Alabama, found that 32 cents of every dollar spent on auto repairs was unnecessary (the figure was 38 cents for women).

With Americans spending an estimated $110.6 billion a year at auto repair shops, annual rip-offs could total *at least* $35 billion.

In addition, the following add even more to the nation's auto repair bills:

- The vast majority of shops charge not by the clock hour, as you might think, but by the often overstated hours listed in price-fixing "flat-rate manuals." This system could easily boost your labor bill by 30 percent or more.
- An estimated 50,000 new vehicles a year turn out to be "lemons"—i.e., substantially defective, according to the Center for Auto Safety. Weaknesses in many state lemon laws mean some vehicles never get repaired properly.
- Used-car dealers often knowingly sell defective cars, including new-car lemons as well as older models reconstructed from wrecks or from flood-damaged inventory.
- New-car dealers gyp many new-car buyers out of hundreds of dollars for questionable and overpriced add-ons, such as service contracts, rustproofing, and paint protection.
- Car makers from time to time have "secret warranties" for defects that crop up after the regular warranty expires. However, only those who complain loudly are let in on the secret and get free repairs; others must pay out of their own pockets. (See *Get Your Car Fixed Free*, Consumer Reports Books, 1994.)
- Some repair shops charge for emission system repairs that auto manufacturers are obligated under federal law to fix for free.
- Auto insurance companies often don't pay body shops enough money to repair cars to precrash condition.

Still to be included in the rip-off total is the additional dollar loss from bad repairs. This includes the need to take time off from work, rental of a replacement car, accident costs, excessive emissions, wasted fuel, depreciation, etc.

The irony is that while all too many repair shops are keen to sell unneeded repairs, they overlook work that actually needs to be done. The Motor and Equipment Manufacturers Association estimates that each year $59.4 billion worth of needed maintenance goes undone.

While the nation's auto repair system is totally in need of a major overhaul, here's what state and local lawmakers have been doing about the problem:

- Only two states and two counties require auto mechanics to pass competency tests (see chapter 6). In the 48 other states, somebody without any training or testing could work on your car.
- Only six states and a handful of cities and counties license and regulate auto repair shops in an attempt to keep them honest. Another five states license body shops only (see chapter 7).
- Only half the states require auto repair shops to give written estimates, return parts, and follow specified procedures to protect consumers (see chapter 7).
- Only four states require manufacturers who take back new-car lemons to fix them correctly before reselling them; some 20 states don't require manufacturers to disclose that they are trying to sell a new-car lemon bought back from the original owner (see chapter 18).
- Only four states require mandatory warranties for certain used cars, and only three have used-car lemon laws (see chapter 21).

With so little help from federal, state, and local governments, consumers must educate themselves to avoid becoming a victim of an auto repair rip-off.

PART I

Rip-offs Galore, and How to Avoid Them

1

Phony Flat-Rate Time.

Here's a real-life math quiz:

A motorist takes his car to a dealer for service. The shop has a posted labor rate of $44 per hour, and the total bill for labor comes to $753.

How long did the shop work on the car?

If you got an answer of 17.11 hours, you would be mathematically correct. However, the actual time spent working on the car was only six hours.

You have just entered the auto repair "twilight zone," where all normal concepts of time are distorted.

Unknown to most consumers, auto repair shops rarely charge by the clock hour. Instead, they typically charge for the amount of time listed in one of several flat-rate manuals. These manuals list various repair operations for each car and then state how long each repair should take. The con: It's quite common for repair times to be overstated by half or more.

In our little quiz, the shop was not charging $44 per hour. For six hours of labor, that would have meant a labor bill of $264. Instead, it was charging $44 per "flat-rate hour."

The difference in the bill: a whopping $489 ($753 minus $264). Thus, the labor rate per real hour was not $44; in this case it was $125.50 per hour ($753 divided by 6 hours of actual labor).

A Naval Academy student had a similar experience when she took her 1991 Honda into a Maryland dealership for a 15,000-mile service. She was charged $204 for four hours of labor even though she handed over the keys at 7:38 A.M. and got the car back at 8:45 A.M.

Types of Manuals

There are essentially three types of auto repair flat-rate manuals, which are computerized as well: (1) those published by the auto manufacturers for their dealers to follow when doing warranty repairs and, in some cases, retail repairs; (2) those designed exclusively for retail customer mechanical repairs; and (3) those for determining crash repair time allowances.

The auto manufacturers supposedly compute their flat-rate manuals by making time-and-motion studies of how long it takes mechanics to perform each repair job on new-model cars. They then base their warranty reimbursements on these labor times in an effort to limit their warranty payments. For example, General Motors allowed 54 minutes of labor to remove, replace, and rebuild the wheel cylinders on its 1993 Chevrolet Celebrity, Buick Century, Oldsmobile Cutlass Ciera and Cutlass Cruiser, and Pontiac 6000. In this case, whether the dealer did the repair in two hours or a half hour, it would be paid for only 54 minutes of labor multiplied by the dealer's hourly labor rate.

That brings us to the second type of flat-rate manual: those put out by independent publishers for dealers and other repair shops to follow when doing retail mechanical work. These include the Chilton, Motor, and Mitchell manuals.

They take the manufacturers' labor times and add to them liberally. For example, instead of allowing 54 minutes to do the same wheel cylinder repairs as prescribed by GM, Chilton allows 1.5 hours, or two-thirds more time. Some additional labor time is justified. As cars get older, it often takes longer to remove rusted bolts, clear accumulated road dirt, and the like. But the independent flat-rate manuals still often overestimate the time needed for repairs.

Multiple Repairs

The use of such manuals often results in even bigger rip-offs when more than one repair is involved. This is true because the time for the mechanic to drive the car into the stall, get out the necessary tools, remove certain parts to get at the repair area, retrieve parts, make the repair, replace any parts that were removed, put the tools away, and drive the car out of the stall is supposedly built into the flat-rate hours for each repair.

However, most shops will not make allowance for those actions if they do more than one repair. They'll just charge you the full flat-rate time for each repair.

For example, a man in Virginia asked a dealer to perform 14 chores on his 1985 Nissan Stanza. In each case, the dealership charged him the full flat-rate time as listed in "the book" —industry lingo for the flat-rate manual. At $52 per flat-rate hour, this added up to $795.15 for labor. Among the charges: one hour to mount and balance two tires and 1.6 hours to replace a muffler.

How lucrative is this rip-off? The New York State attorney general's office surveyed invoices at 21 new-car dealerships, and estimated in 1980 that motorists in the state were being overcharged over $73 million annually through the use of flat-rate manuals.

The third type of flat-rate manual—crash estimators—is used by body shops and insurance companies. Whereas the labor times in these manuals are quite liberal, insurance companies keep down the cost by dictating a relatively low dollar rate per flat-rate hour. Mitchell's crash estimator is considered the leader here.

The Mechanic Connection

As if charging for phony, overinflated hours weren't bad enough, the flat-rate system has even worse repercussions. It may result in fraudulent activities and bad repairs, and discourages competent people from staying in or even entering the auto repair profession. This is because the mechanic's pay is directly linked to flat-rate book time.

Most mechanics are not paid by the clock hour or the week, as you might assume. Instead, they are paid by the flat-rate hour or a low, guaranteed base wage plus flat-rate hours. This means that for each flat-rate hour the shop charges you, the mechanic earns a flat-rate hour of pay.

To illustrate: Let's say you own a 1993 Ford Taurus or Mercury Sable and take it to a repair shop to have the alternator replaced. The mechanic replaces the alternator in 10 minutes, but "Chilton time" for that repair is 42 minutes. The shop charges $50 a flat-rate hour for labor, and so you are charged $35 for labor (seven-tenths of an hour times $50).

However, just as you are charged for 42 minutes of labor even though the mechanic took 10 minutes, the mechanic is paid for 42 minutes of labor even though the work took only 10 minutes. Let's say the mechanic earns $12 for every flat-rate hour billed. In your case, the mechanic would earn $12 multiplied by seven-tenths of an hour, or $8.40 for 10 minutes of work.

Under this setup, a mechanic working on flat-rate (or "piece-work," as it's often called) can accumulate 11, 12, 16, or more flat-rate hours in an eight-hour day. At $12 an hour, as in our example, a mechanic who collected 16 flat-rate hours a day would earn $192 ($12 x 16), whereas one who billed eight flat-rate hours would take home only $96 ($12 x 8).

Using this system, the mechanic is actually encouraged

to cheat you and rush work in an effort to "beat the book" and collect flat-rate hours.

The Cheating Incentive

With their pay directly linked to the labor bill, mechanics have an incentive to sell you repairs you don't need. They're especially encouraged to make those repairs for which "the book" allows extravagant time allowances—a one-hour flat-rate job that takes a few minutes, a three-hour "book" job that takes an hour, and so on.

They also have an incentive to make as many repairs as possible on the car in front of them—to do five repairs to one car rather than one repair to each of five cars. That's because they can pick up the full flat-rate time for each repair without taking the time to move the car, gather and put away tools after each repair, etc.

In the same vein, once a mechanic has taken time to remove some parts to get at a repair, there is a tremendous inducement to replace one or more additional parts in the vicinity. This way, the mechanic can pick up the full flat-rate time for each repair.

Mechanics have another incentive to cheat under the flat-rate system when there's little business in the shop, when they have to do work over again, or when they earn fewer flat-rate hours than clock hours expended on a particular repair.

If business is slow, the flat-rate mechanic might start looking for flat-rate hours to collect from whatever customers do come in. If the mechanic gets a "comeback"—a repair that wasn't done right—the repair must be redone for free without collecting any flat-rate time. The mechanic may then be tempted to try to catch up for lost wages by cheating another customer.

Then there's the possibility a particular repair may prove so difficult and time-consuming that a mechanic spends most or all of one day on it and collects only a few flat-rate hours. To make up for it, the mechanic or the shop might cheat another customer.

In Canada, a service adviser who had been with the same General Motors dealership for nearly 20 years got caught making up a fraudulent warranty work order to cover for a mechanic who earned little on a flat-rate job. The adviser was fired and later sued the dealer for wrongful dismissal, claiming that what he did was commonplace. He lost.

Flat-rate mechanics at new-car dealerships have yet another incentive to cheat: to make up for the difference between so-called factory time and higher retail time.

Using our previous example of the 1993 Ford Taurus and Mercury Sable, a dealer mechanic who replaces the alternator under warranty would be paid for 24 flat-rate minutes of labor, while if the exact same repair for a retail customer were done using the Chilton manual, the mechanic would be paid for 48 flat-rate minutes.

The Flat-Rate System and Incompetence

Flat-rate mechanics are, in effect, paid a low hourly wage and then pressured to earn more by racing against the clock to accumulate lots of flat-rate hours.

Because the manuals basically specify the time to perform specified repairs but say nothing about how long it might take to check out various possibilities before deciding what repair to make, mechanics who take the time to figure out what's wrong aren't rewarded for their time or their skill. Where speed is rewarded more than quality, mechanics known as "parts hangers" are rewarded for their lack of skill. The parts hangers are usually not competent enough to diagnose malfunctions, and so they keep replacing parts until the problem goes away. Of course, each time they replace a part, they're rewarded with flat-rate pay time.

Why Good Mechanics Quit

Some mechanics do very well under the flat-rate system—even honestly—because they do their work fast and efficiently.

Also, most mechanics can beat the flat-rate allowance most of the time. "Show me one flat-rate time allowance that most technicians will not beat by 10 to 20 percent and I will be surprised," says W. J. Buxton, a retired vice president of General Motors.

Nevertheless, the system eventually forces many good

mechanics to leave the business and discourages competent people from entering it. Mechanics don't have to just beat the flat-rate, they've got to beat it by a healthy enough margin to make a good living.

Working against many mechanics are shop inefficiencies that cost them time and thus keep their wages down. The proper tools are not always in the proper place, and the proper parts are not always available.

Sooner or later, many mechanics figure they're not benefiting from the flat-rate system and leave the business or go to work in a fleet shop for a regular salary.

For example, a young mechanic in a large dealership might find that jobs aren't handed out fairly. The older mechanics get all the relatively simple lucrative jobs, while the younger ones are stuck with more difficult, time-consuming repairs. On the other hand, if jobs are handed out evenly, aging mechanics may find they can no longer beat the flat rate as they did in their younger days. Thus, the more experienced they become, the less they may earn.

A mechanic in Colorado said he gave up being an auto mechanic for a career in teaching largely because of the flat-rate pay system. The day he decided to quit was when he found out he was going to be paid only 7.3 hours for changing the timing chain on a 2.3-liter Mercury Topaz, which required removal of the engine and transaxle. He said he didn't mind doing comebacks as a result of his mistakes, but he remembered losing the better part of a day's pay because the parts store sent over the wrong part.

The flat-rate pay system also discourages prospective entrants into the field because it puts a damper on apprenticeship programs. A mechanic who is concerned with beating the book to make a living is not going to want to take time to instruct an apprentice or two.

Is It Legal?

Is the flat-rate system illegal price-fixing? Under the Sherman Antitrust Act, to prove illegal price-fixing one must first prove that the participants contracted, combined, or conspired among one other. From the viewpoint of the flat-rate manual publishers (Capital Cities ABC Inc., Hearst Corp., etc.), they are merely exercising their First Amendment right to publish a book, and repair shops are free to charge for any repair time they wish. Indeed, a consumer class action suit in the 1970s alleged price-fixing in connection with an automobile flat-rate manual, but it was rejected by a federal jury on similar grounds.

The suit alleged that Mercedes-Benz of North America, Inc., and its parent companies conspired with their authorized dealers "to fix, raise, and maintain rates charged for nonwarranty auto repairs performed on Mercedes-Benz automobiles" by basing rates on labor times in what was known as the *MBNA Labor Time Guide.*

The jury, after a seven-week trial, determined that Mercedes's dealers were free to use whatever method they wanted to determine retail repair charges and that no conspiracy existed. The U.S. Court of Appeals in 1986 affirmed that decision.[1]

State Restrictions

Only a few states have laws or regulations concerning flat-rate manuals.

A Wisconsin regulation requires that invoices show the actual time required to complete repairs if units of time based on flat-rate averages are used.

New York State and the city of Chicago require that written estimates must indicate the hourly labor charge and how it's computed, i.e., by clock hours or flat rate. If flat rate, the manual used must be specified and the consumer, upon request, must be shown relevant time rates as listed in the manual. In New York, shops must also post a sign telling how its labor charge is computed.

Prior notification of flat-rate charging is required in Florida; in Montgomery County, Maryland (on written estimates for work over $50 and $25 respectively); and in Maine (on a posted notice). Massachusetts and Montgomery County require invoices to indicate whether hours charged were actual or flat rate.

Defense of the System

Despite all the rip-offs and negative consequences of the flat-rate system, it is still defended by many in the industry.

Many contend that customers are protected because they don't have to pay for labor time exceeding the flat-rate allotment should a repair prove difficult. In truth, many shops try to win both ways. If they can't beat the manual on a particular repair, they might charge you what they feel like charging. If they do repairs in less time than the manual calls for, they charge you the full flat-rate allowance.

Precautions

The best way not to get ripped off by the flat-rate system is to find a shop that doesn't use it—perhaps one that charges by the clock hour, with an up-front diagnostic fee that rewards them for being able to pinpoint the problem immediately. But that's easier said than done.

The next best thing is to make sure, before you contract for a repair, that you understand exactly how the labor charge is to be computed.

Also, ask shops if the mechanics are being paid by flat rate, and try to deal with those that pay by the clock hour or week.

If You Think You've Been Gypped

It may be possible to fight the flat-rate system in small-claims court under state laws prohibiting unfair and deceptive trade practices (see chapter 28), or for violation of the above-mentioned laws and regulations concerning flat-rate charging.

A clear-cut deceptive practice is when the shop posts its labor rate per hour but doesn't disclose that the rate is based on flat-rate hours. Another is if the shop uses the word *hours* in the labor charge section of your invoice and hasn't disclosed to you that it means flat-rate hours.

2

The Transmission
Tricksters

"Something inside your transmission is falling apart."

"Your transmission is cannibalizing itself."

"This transmission is being eaten away inside."

These are just some of the lines used by some automatic transmission mechanics as they show customers the metal filings from their car's transmission oil pan. It's all part of a scam.

"Even a moderate amount of metal particles is normal for most cars," says the Michigan Bureau of Automotive Regulation. "Tiny metal particles in the transmission pan do not necessarily indicate a problem."

Nevertheless, year after year, transmission shops pull the "metal particles" and other tricks on thousands of unsuspecting motorists, making automatic transmissions the biggest single type of repair rip-off. Here's a sampler:

- In the early 1990s, Florida officials closed down a chain called Transmission Kingdom, which had shops in many south Florida cities. Investigators said the chain would lure customers with an advertised $9.95 transmission tune-up that should have retailed for about $35 and then proceed to rip them off. In one instance, a shop told an investigator that there was serious leakage in a transmission and charged $400 for repairs. In fact, the shop only repainted the transmission and didn't even bother to change the old transmission fluid.

- In 1990, Cottman Transmissions, Inc., without admitting guilt, agreed to pay $60,000 in investigative costs to settle charges by the Missouri state attorney general's office. The office had alleged that five franchised Cottman centers recommended major transmission overhauls on undercover cars when only minor repairs, if any, were needed.

- In 1989, New Jersey investigators said they were cheated at 8 of 12 transmission shops visited. Whereas four shops fixed the minor problem at no cost, the others—seven of them franchisees of national chains—said repairs of $125 to $175 were needed. The investigators charged that the seven franchisees, which included three Lee Myles shops, two Gibraltar outlets, one AAMCO shop, and a Cottman facility, all wanted to disassemble the transmission before making a diagnosis.

- In 1988, the Maryland state attorney general's office alleged that 11 of the state's 13 Cottman Transmissions franchisees gouged undercover agents on 17 of 22 visits made between June 1986 and June 1987. On 12 occasions, investigators said, they were sold major transmission repairs on properly working cars. The average bill was $617. On three other occasions, they were charged $695 to $876 for overhauls that were not performed. Cottman was fined $100,000.

The Cottman Way

Whereas there are many independent shops, new-car dealers, and regional chains that practice automatic transmission thievery, some of the biggest scamsters seem to come out of the highly advertised national franchise organizations.

The Maryland state attorney general's investigation into Cottman Transmissions, Inc., a franchisor in some 20 states, gives a startling look into that segment of the transmission business. "Cottman preferred to sell its franchises to those persons who had no prior experience in this business," says Maryland attorney general Joseph Curran, Jr. Why? They "did not want to have people who really knew the business," says Curran. "They wanted to be able to teach them."

Did they teach them how to repair transmissions? Not really. Maryland investigators found that during a three-week training program for new franchisees, almost all of the time was devoted to selling transmissions. Only about a half day was devoted to learning how to fix them. Indeed, the training was more like a theater course than a repair course. Much of the three weeks, investigators found, was devoted to learning a sales script word for word and then playacting with other trainees. After an inspection, the trainees were taught to say they couldn't determine the problem or the price until after tearing down the transmission.

In court testimony, Cottman vice president James Corkran admitted that after inspecting a transmission and doing a road test, a transmission shop knows with 99 percent certainty whether a so-called soft parts overhaul is needed.

Nevertheless, only after customers had committed themselves to anywhere from $85 to $500 for the teardown were they told of the need for an overhaul and the price—which ranged from $650 to $1,000, according to Curran. If they elected not to have repairs done, they would be charged the teardown cost and still have an inoperative car.

Curran said that if customers had known beforehand what it would cost, they may not have elected to have an older car repaired or they could have gotten a second opinion before committing themselves to a teardown. (Once customers have agreed to a teardown, the shop usually further entices them into an expensive rebuilding job by offering to forget about the teardown charge if repairs are authorized.)

Maryland investigators even found a videotaped survey that Cottman did in Virginia to determine what would happen if they told customers about a rebuilding job up front. When they were truthful, only 12 percent agreed to repairs. However, when they concealed the truth, 90 percent agreed to a teardown.

Investigators also learned that Cottman, which got many of its customers by heavily advertising a free courtesy check, had a quota system in which they expected 6 out of every 10 customers to be sold an overhauled transmission. The company then took 20.5 percent of each franchisee's gross sales for itself.

Why do people frequent these franchised shops if so many of them have been guilty of questionable business practices? It would seem that it all has to do with advertising.

Michigan state attorney general Frank Kelley says consumers tend to visit repair shops not because of local reputation or past dealings but because of the lure of advertising claims. This, he says, enables national chains to engage in nationwide fraud.

Loss-leader ads or coupons offering low cost repairs, free diagnosis, or free towing—coupled with commission systems and absentee ownership at many franchised shops—are a sure formula for trouble, say Florida officials.

The FTC and AAMCO

Nationally, franchised chains have been able to thrive over the past 30 years while engaging in scandalous behavior—largely because the Federal Trade Commission (FTC) has seemingly chosen to look the other way. Also, present federal law makes it difficult to go after franchisors.

The FTC, for example, has not prevented the AAMCO organization from continuing its questionable business practices. An FTC staff investigation of AAMCO in the years after the organization's incorporation in 1963 found that AAMCO Transmissions, Inc., the franchisor, encouraged its franchisees to sell rebuilt transmissions to everyone whether they needed them or not and engaged in "bait and switch" advertising, according to a staff memo. The FTC also alleged that many AAMCO franchisees would get customers to pay for a teardown and then afterward, if they balked at an expensive rebuilding job, would tell them it would cost more money to have their transmission reassembled.

In a 1970 consent agreement, the FTC got AAMCO (which did not admit guilt) to agree that, among other things, it would not engage in deceptive advertising or sales practices, that the charge for removing and tearing down a transmission would include the cost of reassembly as well, and that it would sell only those parts and services that were actually needed.

However, the consent order didn't require AAMCO to reveal the cost of rebuilding a transmission before tearing it down, even though the franchisees knew all along what that cost would be. It could be argued that it also practically exonerated AAMCO Transmissions, Inc., and its owner, Robert Morgan, from the activities of its franchisees. It allowed AAMCO to police its own franchisees to make sure they followed FTC-imposed guidelines.

Not only that, but a provision in the agreement said that AAMCO didn't even have to investigate a franchisee unless it got 18 or more complaints against that franchisee *within a calendar year*.

Despite continued deceptive practices within the AAMCO organization, the FTC has taken no further action since 1970. As a result, state and local governments have had to pick up the slack.

From 1970 to 1984, over 45 AAMCO shops were caught selling or trying to sell unnecessary repairs—usually involving hundreds of dollars—by at least 16 state and local law enforcement agencies, the news media, and Better Business Bureaus (BBBs). At least eight of the shops and/or their employees were convicted of criminal activities, and AAMCO and its franchisees paid over $232,000 in penalties to state and local governments.

In a 1981 probe, for example, the California Bureau of Automotive Repair said it sent 22 undercover cars into AAMCO shops statewide and got ripped off 16 times. As a result, nine franchisees, without admitting guilt, paid $100,000 in penalties. In 1983 and 1984, the operators of six AAMCO shops in southern California had their licenses revoked by the Bureau of Automotive Repair. However, it wasn't until a probe by 14 state attorneys general ending in 1987 that AAMCO's business was impacted. AAMCO Transmissions, Inc., without admitting guilt, paid $500,000 in penalties and agreed to give customers in the 14 states firm prices for rebuilding transmissions prior to disassembling them.

AAMCO went so far as to put out deceptive information after its agreement with each attorney general. The company explained that the language of the agreements meant that allegations involving AAMCO were without basis. Actually, the agreements said nothing of the kind. The AAMCO releases also stated that the money paid to each attorney general was for the cost of developing a dispute-settling program. In reality, about half of the $500,000 went to the cost of the investigation, including the use of undercover cars.

Legislation Needed

To better regulate auto repair franchisors, Maryland attorney general Curran would like to see Congress amend the Lanham Act, which deals with trademarks. He wants to make a franchisor selling auto repair services "equally liable with its franchisees for any unfair, fraudulent, or deceptive conduct" engaged in by franchisees in dealing with consumers. This, he said, would give franchisors an economic incentive to clean up their shops.

Trade Regulation

The FTC has failed to combat fraudulent practices within the automatic transmission industry with any kind of trade regulation. California, for example, requires shops to reveal the following prior to disassembling a transmission: (1) the cost of installing a rebuilt replacement and torque converter or rebuilding the transmission, (2) the cost to reassemble the transmission without fixing it, and (3) the terms of any warranty in effect.

Avoiding Rip-offs

To avoid being ripped off by automatic transmission shops, you need to take many precautions .

"Your best bet," says the Michigan Bureau of Automotive Regulation, "is to invest in inexpensive routine maintenance and get at least two written estimates if repairs are recommended." Routine maintenance, according to the bureau, does not require a specialist. It consists of periodically checking the quality of the transmission fluid, refilling the fluid if necessary, and having the transmission screen or filter cleaned or replaced. According to the bureau, a more detailed inspection service by transmission shops should include a fluid-level check, test drive, manual-linkage check, oil-pan removal, band adjustment, and screen cleaning or filter replacement. The oil pan is usually removed and inspected for metal particles and friction material.

Be leery, however, of any shop that advertises or offers low-cost transmission-maintenance specials.

You should maintain the proper transmission-fluid level, change the fluid at the recommended intervals, and keep your engine cooling system in good order. (The latter is necessary because transmission fluid runs through piping in the radiator to keep it cool.)

The next precaution is never to assume you have a transmission problem. Many people fall into the clutches of unscrupulous transmission shops when their problem could have been solved by a regular mechanic. The Better Business Bureau (BBB) points out, for example, that three engine malfunctions can cause late transmission shifting and clunking as the transmission downshifts when the vehicle slows down: a leak in the vacuum hoses connecting the engine and the transmission, improper adjustment of the engine carburetor throttle linkage, and retarded engine ignition timing setting.

According to the BBB, harsh and rough shifting and rapid shifting in which one gear changes right after the other in quick succession are symptoms of engine vacuum or throttle problems and should be inexpensive to repair. Likewise, lack of a passing gear when you press down quickly on the accelerator pedal usually involves a simple adjustment to the accelerator pedal linkage or adjusting or replacing an electrical switch connected to the accelerator pedal, says the BBB.

Before you authorize any transmission repairs, be sure the shop writes down the symptoms as you describe them on an estimate form. Many motorists pay hundreds of dollars to have their transmission rebuilt, only to find out that the same problem exists afterward. If you want to get your money back in such a situation, you'll need evidence that the work didn't cure the problem.

Your next line of defense is to immediately get your car out of any transmission shop that wants to disassemble your transmission without giving you a firm price on a rebuilding job and the guarantee that comes with it.

If you have had no transmission problems before you came into the shop, be especially dubious when the mechanic says that a teardown is needed. In such a scenario, says the Michigan Bureau of Automotive Regulation, insist on a written explanation why the teardown is necessary—and get a second opinion before authorizing a teardown.

Next, if you suspect a scam and the car is undrivable, pay to have your car towed elsewhere. In 1985 a woman took her 1984 Chevrolet Cavalier to a Cottman Transmissions center because of gear problems. There, mechanics removed and dismantled the transmission and said it needed to be overhauled for $900 to $1,100. Unwilling to pay such a steep bill, the woman had her car towed to a nearby Chevrolet dealer, where mechanics, without removing the transmission, fixed the car for $118.76, including the towing charge.

Also be on the lookout for misrepresentations about the color of transmission fluid.

"Healthy fluid is clear and has a pink or reddish tint," says the BBB. Dark brown liquid exuding a burnt odor indicates that the transmission is slipping. Foamy or milky fluid—also an indication of slippage—is caused by water and coolant leaking from the engine cooling system into the transmission fluid tube.

It's especially important to attend to a transmission leak. If it's caught early, you can limit repairs to either a front or rear seal replacement, says the BBB. However, if a leak continues, resulting low fluid levels could cause extensive damage to your transmission.

Finally, and most important, avoid franchised transmission shops and other highly advertised shops unless you personally know that a particular shop is honest and does good work. Why trust your car to someone who may have answered a business opportunity ad proclaiming "no mechanic experience necessary"?

Your best bet is to do business with a shop owner who has spent his or her working life repairing transmissions and is a member of the Automatic Transmission Rebuilders Association (ATRA), Automotive Service Association (ASA), or other professional trade group.

Also, look for mechanics certified in automatic transmission repair by the National Institute for Automotive Service Excellence (ASE).

3

The Dealer Maintenance Scam

One of the marvels of modern cars is that they need far less preventive maintenance than cars of old.

Oil-change intervals have been lengthened to 7,500 miles or more; grease jobs are usually a thing of the past because of improved suspension systems; and tune-ups are generally needed only every 30,000 to 50,000 miles and often involve only a change of spark plugs (a computer automatically adjusts everything else).

This, in turn, has meant lost maintenance revenue for new-car dealers. But don't fear. Many dealers have found a way to undo progress and undo your wallet in the process.

When you come in for your car's periodic maintenance, dealers may present you with an official-looking maintenance schedule, complete with the auto manufacturer's logo. However, such schedules often far exceed the manufacturer's recommended intervals and are simply a rip-off.

How widespread is this scam? A 1992 survey by *U.S. News & World Report* of 122 dealers for six car makes in Philadelphia, Miami, Chicago, Denver, Dallas, Los Angeles, and Seattle found that nearly 80 percent of the dealers performed more services than the manufacturers recommended, and 63 percent replaced parts the factories insisted did not need replacing.

Whereas the survey turned up lots of needed replacements performed prematurely, it also uncovered what it called "ghost services" and "services of dubious value under any circumstances."

Ghost services, the magazine said, consisted of work on parts that either don't need attention, can't be serviced, "or may not even exist." For example, the survey found that 29 percent of Mazda dealers charged for adjusting the valves at 15,000 miles and 38 percent charged for doing it at 30,000 miles, even though Mazda says the valves are self-adjusting. Other ghost services included chassis lubrication, when in fact the suspension bearings and ball joints were sealed; adjusting the timing or idle speed, both of which were computer-controlled; and cleaning and adjusting the choke on fuel-injected cars, which have no choke.

Services of dubious value included supplementing new oil with chemical additives and flushing fuel injectors that already worked fine.

Of the six car models used in the survey—Honda Accord, Ford Taurus, Saturn, Dodge Caravan, Mazda Miata, and Lexus LS 400—Honda dealers were the only ones to add chargeable services to the factory schedule 100 percent of the time during 15,000- and 30,000-mile services. Almost all of the Honda dealers replaced parts early as well. Coming out best overall were Lexus dealers. At the 15,000-mile interval, *only* 42 percent added services and *only* 16 percent replaced parts early.

On top of that, the magazine found what it called "another bill booster"—overstated labor times. At a dealership in Colorado, total flat-rate labor time for a 30,000-mile inspection came to 5.8 hours—about two hours more than the magazine says can be justified. This included two hours of factory-specified services, with the rest going for replacing the brake fluid and fuel filter; rotating the tires; putting in oil, fuel, and coolant additives; and inspecting the suspension and driveshaft.

The excuse many dealers give for their excesses is that owner's manuals really have two maintenance schedules—one for "normal" and one for "severe" driving conditions. Severe driving might include towing a trailer, lots of hot-weather stop-and-go driving, frequent trips of under 10 miles in freezing weather, driving on dusty roads, etc.

But *U.S. News & World Report* got the same argument about harsh weather everywhere except Los Angeles. It was either heat, cold, humidity, or dryness that necessitated increased maintenance. Stop-and-go driving was cited in every city except Seattle. Some dealers in Philadelphia, Miami, and Chicago said their cities had the worst-quality fuel in the country and this justified increased service. Denver dealers cited their high altitude as an excuse for monitoring fuel-injection systems more closely. Los Angeles dealers cited the smog as a reason for not following factory schedules.

But auto manufacturers are not buying these arguments. Mazda Motors of America, for example, told *U.S. News* that extremely humid climates, to them, were not those of Miami or Houston but of equatorial areas and island countries.

Protecting Yourself

Your best defense against periodic maintenance rip-offs is to check your owner's manual and instruct the dealer to do only what is listed for the particular mileage. If you're not sure whether you do "normal" or "severe" driving, you might allow the dealer to follow the severe-driving conditions intervals and only that.

It surely can't hurt to change your engine oil and filter according to the severe schedules. Many mechanics do so on their own cars, contending that it helps the engine last longer.

Remember: If you don't trust your dealer, you don't need to get maintenance done there or even use the manufacturer's brand-name parts to keep up your warranty. Instead, you can go to an independent shop. Under a federal law, the Magnuson-Moss Warranty–Federal Trade Commission Improvement Act, no warrantor of a consumer product can require you to use any product or service identified by brand, trade, or corporate name unless it's provided free of charge under the terms of the warranty. The only exception is if the FTC grants a waiver based on the fact that only a particular product or service will enable the warranted product to function properly.

If you do get your new car serviced at an independent shop or even at a quickie oil change place, you will need to have proof that you maintained your vehicle according to the manufacturer's schedule to avoid warranty hassles. Make sure all parts and products used meet the manufacturer's specifications, and get legible receipts showing services performed, brand names, parts numbers, the date, and the mileage on your vehicle. Record this information as well in the service log in your owner's manual or warranty booklet.

When choosing a dealer for your maintenance, avoid those that charge high flat rates for this service. It doesn't take a master mechanic to change your oil and rotate your tires.

If you've been the victim of a maintenance scam, you can sue the dealer in small-claims court using your state's unfair and deceptive trade practices law (see chapter 29). You might also wish to include the manufacturer in the suit and let it and the dealer fight things out between themselves. You should argue that either the manufacturer misrepresented the service intervals or the dealer is misrepresenting them. Either way, you may win. Also, complain to your state attorney general's office, which can sue under these laws and may be able to get you a refund as well as put a stop to the scam.

If any dealer insists that you must have maintenance done there to keep up your warranty, have them put it in writing and then report the dealer to the FTC (see Appendix).

4

The Chain Store Massacre

When California officials announced in 1992 that they were thinking of permanently closing down Sears, Roebuck and Company's 72 auto repair centers in the state for badly ripping off state auto repair investigators, it didn't shock those familiar with the industry. Sears and many other famous-name auto repair chains and franchise organizations had been caught by law-enforcement agencies cheating the public before.

Indeed, the household-name national and regional chains may be among the biggest scam artists of them all, with problems stretching back at least 30 years. It appears many of these companies are more in the business of aggressively selling automotive parts than fixing what's actually wrong with your car.

The unfair practices of some companies have given rise to a special jargon. There are, for example, "quotas" in which shops and mechanics are pressured by managers to sell so many specific parts or services within a particular time frame. There are "conversion rates"—a figure closely watched by money-crunchers at corporate headquarters to make sure an expected number of customers coming in for one repair or service are sold a related repair or service. Also part of the lingo is "bogeys"—a billing amount that mechanics must exceed in order to begin receiving commissions.

All too often these and other unfamiliar terms add up to one well-known term: rip-off.

Replacing parts before it is necessary is commonplace. Law enforcement is spotty in most states, and these large chains usually have little to worry about.

Even in California, where repair shops are licensed and regulated, where undercover cars are used frequently to ferret out crooked shops, and where fines can be brutal, the large chains seem to fear not. They seem to merely write off any fines—no matter how large—as a cost of doing business.

This time around, though, Sears seemed to outdo the rest. Between December 1990 and January 1992, California investigators paid 38 visits to Sears auto repair centers and said they found incidences of overselling 90 percent of the time. After warning Sears, another 10 undercover runs were performed in which overselling was found some 70 percent of the time. The average overcharge per shop in the initial investigation was about $245, with a shop in Concord peddling $585 in needless repairs, according to the state's Bureau of Automotive Repair.

To keep its auto repair shops operating in California, Sears paid $8 million—$3.5 million for legal fees and investigative costs, $3 million in restitution payments to customers, and $1.5 million to community college auto repair training programs to buy equipment and supplies.

Nationally, Sears Tire and Auto Centers—which reportedly had annual sales in 1991 of $2.8 billion—paid out some $15 million in cash and coupons to settle charges brought by 42 states and 19 related class action suits. The coupons, valued at $50, went to Sears customers who were sold shock absorbers, coil springs, brake calipers, idler arms, and master cylinders.

These charges brought forth former Sears mechanics to relate their stories. One had worked in Sears auto centers for 16 years and was a service adviser at the Sears center in Canoga Park, California. He filed suit in 1993, alleging that his supervisors "required him to sell a daily quota of regular shock absorbers, MacPherson struts, transmission services . . . alignments, complete brake jobs, oil changes, and a full set of tires to customers" regardless of whether their vehicles required them.

This sort of quota selling, however, is no recent phenomenon —it has been going on for a long time, and certainly has not been confined only to Sears.

The Oregon state attorney general's office interviewed a man in 1973 who had been employed as a mechanic 10 years earlier at a Firestone Tire & Rubber Company store. He said in a signed statement: "They came and would say we have a quota to meet, so many brake shoes, so many tires. . . . I had so many [ball joints] to sell per month. There was an implied directive to either sell them or lose your job."

He claimed he was fired after he refused his boss's order to put new brake shoes on a car that had perfectly good ones.

In 1973 (see comment on page 36), an investigator for the Santa Barbara district attorney's office interviewed a mechanic who had worked for a Goodyear Tire & Rubber Company auto service center for more than two years and left because, as he put it, he was tired of "screwing the public."

He told of competition being set up between various stores, with monthly quotas set. Another former Goodyear employee explained that his store was assigned a quota by the area manager and that the store manager in turn assigned him a quota.

More recently, a certified master mechanic from Tucson claimed he was fired as a Firestone store manager in 1989 "because I refused to participate in the illegal activities as directed by upper management." The mechanic said it was "Firestone policy/practice to assign stores, and for the stores to then assign employees, specific quotas on particular items/ parts." He said, for instance, that if he assigned a salesperson a quota of six shocks or struts a day, it presented a "temptation to suggest to a customer that their old shocks are bad." This, he said, "led to a great deal of questionable shock sales."

A federal consumer class action suit filed in Texas in 1993 alleged that Kmart mechanics were forced to meet quotas or face pay reductions or termination. The court ruled that it lacked jurisdiction, and the suit has since been refiled in state courts in Texas and Oklahoma.

Conversion Rate

In tandem with quotas is the "conversion rate." This practice was explained by a Sears executive at a congressional hearing in 1992.

Jim Thornton, national business manager of Sears's automotive division, said of those who buy tires that his company expects to sell brakes to 40 percent of them and front end parts to 25 percent of them. But he denied that the company forced its employees to adhere to these percentages.

In fact, through it all, Sears has remained rather unrepentant about its practices. When Albert Dombrowski, automotive vice president of the Sears Merchandise Group, spoke at an industry luncheon in 1992, he described Sears's practice of retiring parts before their time as "preventive maintenance," according to *National Petroleum News*. A Sears spokeswoman told the *Washington Post*: "We do not have sales quotas. We have sales goals."

Commissions Are the Culprit

Many consumer protection officials believe that commission systems at the chain stores—for both service advisers and mechanics—are the heart of the problem.

In fact, Sears's troubles really began when it cut hourly wages of mechanics and replaced them with commissions.

California officials said the move resulted in a 50 percent increase in complaints against Sears. Investigators said that before mechanics at one Sears store could receive a commission, they were required to sell five front-end alignments, eight sets of springs, eight sets of shock absorbers, and two tires on each working day.

While Sears did eliminate its service adviser commissions, it continued to pay its mechanics a base salary plus flat-rate commission. A Sears mechanic in California explained in 1992 that it was the mechanics, not the service advisers, who were most capable of diagnosing problems and recommending repairs. Thus, the repairs the service advisers sold to the customer were largely "based on the recommendations of mechanics who are on commission," he said. By 1994, Sears was again using commissions for what it called service "consultants."

In New York the State Consumer Protection Board in 1992 called for the outlawing of commissions in auto repair shops. It surveyed 14 national chain and franchise organizations and said customers may be paying for unneeded repairs because 12 of the chains paid mechanics, service writers, or store managers a commission or bonus based on the amount of work they sold.

Indeed, Goodyear's commission system was blamed by reporters from the *Record* of Hackensack, New Jersey, for giant rip-offs in 1987 and 1988 at a Goodyear repair center in nearby Paramus. That center proposed the most unwarranted repairs of 33 shops visited. On three trips to the shop, the newspaper said it got recommendations for $547 in unnecessary repairs.

The newspaper learned that Goodyear mechanics were paid an hourly wage, but if they exceeded a weekly amount of billings—their "bogey"—they could begin earning a 13.8 percent commission. Goodyear cut out mechanic commissions nationally in mid-1994, after TV exposés of overselling practices.

In addition to paying commissions to staff, franchised shops of national chains themselves have to pay a percentage of sales to the franchisors. According to *The Rating Guide to Franchisors*, Midas franchisees pay a monthly 5 percent royalty and a 5 percent advertising fee, while Meineke Discount Mufflers franchisees pay a hefty monthly 7 percent royalty and a 10 percent advertising fee.

Perception vs. Reality

Many people patronize auto repair chains because of low-priced specials or the perception that prices are lower.

In reality, the chains are often the highest-priced places to get your car repaired. That's because the low advertised prices are often used just to get you into the shop. Afterward, mechanics can sell you additional repairs that may be either unneeded or overpriced. The main "hook" is often a low-priced brake pad, alignment, or muffler special.

Consumer surveys on brakes and muffler repairs at chain shops show that huge numbers of customers find discrepancies between advertised prices and the final bill (see chapters 10, 16, and 32).

According to a diagnostic center report by the University of Alabama at Huntsville, chains may view customers "as very occasional ones who have no loyalty to their shop"—an attitude that isn't likely to generate a positive approach to the consumer. By contrast, service stations, car dealers, and independent shops "generally depend upon goodwill and performance to draw their customers back," the report said.

Indeed, after the Sears fiasco, California officials announced two major busts of highly advertised tire chains in 1993 for similar types of overselling:

Winston Tire Company, with 163 repair centers in the state, paid $1.4 million to settle allegations that it oversold repairs to undercover agents on 32 of 40 trips into 37 different shops. The average charge for work not needed and in some cases not done was about $125.21 per customer, the state's Bureau of Automotive Repair said. The settlement, made without admitting guilt, included $450,000 for restitution to about 20,000 customers.

The operator of 19 Big O Tire Company franchises paid $169,000 in penalties and costs to settle allegations that it badly ripped off undercover investigators. The Orange County district attorney's office, which took cars into five shops owned by the franchisee, said it was sold an average of nearly $400 in unneeded repairs. The franchisee, CSB Partnership, did not admit guilt.

The Power of Advertising

The power of auto repair chain advertising to lure the public can be seen in the case of Midas International Corp., the muffler and brake shop chain, a subsidiary of Whitman Corporation.

In 1993, Midas launched a $50 million advertising campaign. The purpose was to try to convince the public that the organization was trustworthy, even though recent undercover operations in Pennsylvania had shown otherwise. The campaign used letters from people who had had bad experiences at other shops and came to Midas, where their problems were solved.

A Midas radio commercial in 1994 went so far as to claim that at Midas, "it's fixing only what needs fixing. Most of all it's proving a car repair company can be honest." This came after Bruce Chelberg, the chairman of Whitman Corporation, said in a 1993 interview with Reuters that Midas's earnings in 1992 were flat in part because some Midas franchisees were reluctant to push certain services. If they tried to do so, he said, it might be construed as misleading in light of the Sears crackdown.

A lot of the advertising money of some big auto repair organizations may well come from overselling practices and/or high prices. It's a self-perpetuating system where customers pay for advertising to attract even more customers. This often ends up corrupting independent shops because it induces many of them to engage in the same practices.

Positive Aspects

Despite all the negatives to be found with the chains, there is a positive side. The chains may guarantee both parts and labor and have a policy of giving written estimates—something many shops don't do unless required by law.

William Arendt, chief of the division of vehicle safety in New York's Department of Motor Vehicles, says the number of complaints against the big chains is minor relative to their total volume of business. He says chain mechanics might even be better trained at minor repairs than those at other shops, since at least they have lots of cars on which to practice. He warns, however, that chain mechanics might not be knowledgeable enough to do engine analysis and more difficult repairs.

It must also be emphasized that not all chains are corrupt. And not all shops are dishonest within chains cited for corruption. It is also true that chains may have both honest and crooked franchisees.

The Failure of the Feds

Because these companies operate nationally or in more than one state, the chain problem is well within the jurisdiction of the Federal Trade Commission.

Since the late 1970s, the FTC has been aware of national chain store rip-offs—thanks to federal diagnostic center reports and investigations by various law enforcement agencies around the country. Yet the agency has done nothing to stop them.

In California alone, sleuthing by various district attorneys over the years has resulted in some eye-popping settlements for alleged auto repair rip-offs. To wit: Goodyear, 1973, $80,000 (Santa Barbara County); Sears, 1987, $80,000 (Orange County); Kmart, 1978, $93,492 (Alameda County); Firestone, 1983, $150,000 (Ventura County); Montgomery Ward, 1983, $80,864 (Stanislaus County) and 1985, $110,000 (El Dorado County); Midas (3 franchises), 1989, $360,000 (Alameda, San Francisco, San Mateo, and Santa Clara counties). Here's a sampling of just some of the more recent state and local investigations into particular chains.

Midas

1994. The New York state attorney general's office forced Midas to stop low-price advertising, which it said was designed to lure customers into Midas shops only to be hit with unexpectedly high repair bills. Investigators said only 5 percent of Midas's customers came away with an advertised $24.95 "economizer" muffler, whereas the average customer paid more than four times as much. Only 12 percent paid the usual $59 or $69 for advertised brake jobs. Midas, which admitted no guilt, agreed to pay $50,000 in investigative costs and to advertise prices only if at least 65 percent of customers' bills do not exceed the advertised price by 15 percent.

1993. The operators of 12 franchised Midas shops in the Pittsburgh area paid $51,250 to settle charges brought by the Pennsylvania state attorney general's office. The Midas outlets, which admitted no guilt, were accused of recommending and performing costly, unnecessary repairs or failing to detect serious problems during safety inspections. The allegations stemmed from a major sting operation involving city and state police and the attorney general's office.

1992. A Midas Muffler shop in Philadelphia owned by Cosmic Enterprises Inc. (a Midas subsidiary) admitted no guilt, but paid $10,000 in civil penalties and costs to settle allegations brought by the Pennsylvania state attorney general's office. The office said it did an undercover operation at four company-owned shops in the Philadelphia area and that one of them recommended $452 in unneeded repairs.

1989. Three separate owners of four Midas shops in Philadelphia and Abington, Pennsylvania, paid $7,000 in penalties and costs to settle allegations that they performed or recommended unneeded brake repairs on cars brought in by the state attorney general undercover operatives. One of the outlets was owned by Cosmic Enterprises Inc.

Sears

1992. New Jersey investigators made two undercover car runs against each of six Sears auto repair centers and said they got recommendations for unneeded repairs each time ranging from $30 to $406. Sears's average rip-off was $341. As part of the settlement, Sears paid $200,000 to underwrite a National Association of Attorneys General auto repair study and also paid $3,000 in penalties.

The Pennsylvania state attorney general's office accused Sears of deceptive advertising for a brake special. The ad in question contained a coupon to replace front disc brakes for $48 on "most cars/light trucks" and noted "semi-metallic material and imports extra."

The scam: An estimated 88 to 92 percent of all vehicles in Pennsylvania required semi-metallic brake pads and therefore weren't eligible for the sale price. In some cases, Sears charged an extra $10 to $20 to install semi-metallic pads, investigators said. Sears, without admitting any wrongdoing, agreed to pay $4,000 in investigative costs, make restitution of $20 each to 219 customers, and change its advertising practices nationwide.

Goodyear

1994. After hearing allegations from Goodyear mechanics about overselling practices, WMAQ-TV in Chicago sent three cars into 13 Goodyear-owned repair centers and asked for an inspection prior to going on a trip. Each car was in tip-top shape except for an induced defect. Three shops did a total of $1,162 in allegedly unnecessary work, and another three gave estimates of $500 to $655 for work that an AAA Chicago Motor Club consultant said was not needed.

1992. KSTP-TV in St. Paul, Minnesota, made 10 visits to Goodyear-owned shops and said the company tried to sell it unneeded repairs on all but one occasion. On a visit for a free brake inspection, one shop wanted to do $330 worth of brake work, including new rotors. Another Goodyear store said the existing rotors were fine. During a $17 oil change, one shop wanted to do some $500 in work, including new shocks and struts. When the same car with different license plates and driver was taken back to the shop, the driver was told that the shocks and struts were okay but that the car had a $500 clutch problem. The TV station's mechanical expert said the clutch was fine.

1989. A Goodyear store in Upper Darby, Pennsylvania, paid $2,500 in penalties to settle charges it sold or recommended unnecessary brake repairs during a state-run undercover operation.

5

Beware of Ronald Reagan Bumpers

This is the story of Ronald Reagan bumpers and "trickle-up economics."

Ronald Reagan bumpers, in case you weren't aware, are those put on cars after 1982, when the Reagan administration lowered the speed at which bumpers must protect cars in front and rear barrier crashes.

The standard speed that had applied to the 1980-82 model years—5 mph—was reduced to 2.5 mph. Although the previous regulation had allowed only minor, cosmetic damages to the bumpers themselves, the new rule permitted unlimited damage.

Pendulum impact standards were also lowered—from 5 mph to 2.5 mph for front and rear impacts, and from 3 mph to 1.5 mph for corner impacts.

The result: The automobile companies have gotten richer while, according to Brian O'Neill, president of the Insurance Institute for Highway Safety (IIHS), customers "have paid and paid and paid again."

For example, here's what the IIHS found when it crash-tested nine 1993 midsize four-door cars at 5 mph: In front-into-barrier crashes, they incurred from $229 to $801 in damage. In rear-into-barrier crashes, two cars—the Dodge Spirit and Honda Civic—showed no damage, whereas the others incurred from $96 to $1,041 in damage (see Table 5.1, p. 47).

Indeed, while the 1980s and 1990s have seen an explosion of forward-looking auto technology, bumper technology has gone backward. Whereas the 1981 Ford Escort sustained no damage in the required 5-mph front and rear barrier tests as well as in more demanding 5-mph front-angle barrier and rear pole tests, no car since has had a perfect score on all four tests. In fact, the 1992 Mitsubishi Eclipse was the first car in more than a decade that had no damage in the front-angle barrier test.

Of the 1993 midsize models tested, damage in the front-angle barrier test ran from $360 for the Dodge Spirit to $1,669 for the Toyota Camry LE; rear (into pole) damage ranged from $609 for the Saturn SL2 to $1,879 for the Mercury Sable GS.

In crash tests of 1994 passenger vans, damage to the Mazda MPV was a whopping $2,080 at 5-mph front-angle barrier and $3,179 rear-into-pole tests at 5 mph. In fact, the Mazda couldn't be driven after the front-angle barrier test. Passenger van bumpers are not required to meet any federal standards.

At such low speeds, these are the kinds of bumps that might occur in a parking lot. According to a 1991 IIHS study of cars brought to drive-in claim centers in Chicago, Houston, Los Angeles, and Washington, DC, about one-fifth of auto insurance claims for damage involve parking lot collisions.

Rollback Reasoning

The rationale behind the 1982 rollback was that it would lower car prices and reduce bumper weight, which in turn would conserve fuel. The savings, it was argued, would more than offset the cost of any increased damage. Also, the Reagan administration promised it was going to begin a program of informing consumers of the relative merits of different bumper systems.

All these assertions were riding on empty.

"There is no evidence that reduced bumper protection has significantly reduced car prices or weights or improved fuel economy," says IIHS president O'Neill. Meanwhile, he added, "Insurance collision claim frequencies have sharply increased for cars with weakened bumpers."

Clarence M. Ditlow III, director of the Center for Auto Safety, says the "only thing consumers ever got was large repair bills for accidents at speeds no faster than a toddler walks."

Look at these facts:

- *Car prices were not lowered.* Chrysler, for example, weakened the bumpers on some of its 1983 models after the model year had begun and charged exactly the same price for the cars. They simply removed the energy absorbers from the bumpers and replaced them with rigid mounting brackets designed to absorb crash energy by bending and sustaining damage.
- *There have been little or no fuel savings.* Ditlow says that the Center for Auto Safety looked at identical cars with and without 5-mph bumpers and found that they had the same fuel mileage rating.
- *There is no definite correlation between bumper weight and damage resistance.* The Honda Accord, with relatively light bumpers, performed best among 22 1991 midsize four-door cars tested by IIHS. The Subaru Legacy, on the other hand, had among the heaviest bumpers and performed among the worst.
- *The federal government never provided comparison information on bumpers.* It wasn't until the 1994 model

year that the Big-Three automakers began voluntarily providing labels on their cars about the bumpers' ability to withstand low-speed crashes.

To defend its decision for rolling back the standards, in 1989 the National Highway Traffic Safety Administration (NHTSA) sent Barry Felrice, the agency's associate administrator for rule-making, before a U.S. Senate subcommittee.

Felrice said the agency did an evaluation of 1983–84 cars and figured that consumers would save $8 in 1984 dollars on re-duced bumper standards over the lifetime of their car. Repair costs, according to Felrice, would increase by $36, which would be more than compensated by a $44 reduction in bumper and fuel costs. Included in his calculation was only $4 for the delay and inconvenience of getting the car repaired.

Felrice said that when the NHTSA changed the rule, it esti-mated about two-thirds of crashes that occur under 5 mph also occur under 2.5 mph, and that crashes between 2.5 and 5 mph would occur only once every 40 car years—or about one car out of four in 10 years. "Everyone would pay for the higher protec-tion, but few people would actually benefit from that protection," he said.

Senator Richard H. Bryan of Nevada called Felrice's testimony "rather bizarre." Senator John C. Danforth of Missouri ques-tioned Felice's premise that 5-mph bumpers would protect cars only in crashes between 2.5 mph and 5 mph and not at higher speeds. O'Neill said crash tests of cars with 5-mph bumpers in earlier years showed they were effective in preventing or mini-mizing damage to such components as exhaust, brake, steering, cooling, and fuel systems in 10- and 15-mph crashes.

Senator Danforth also disputed the $8 savings for the lower bumper standard, contending that higher insurance costs would quickly eat up the difference. (The lowering of the 5-mph standard was felt immediately in the increased number of insurance collision claims. They shot up dramatically on some 1984 models with weaker bumpers, compared with 1983 mod-els with 5-mph bumpers. Collision claims for the Buick Electra, for example, soared 29 percent.)

Clarence Ditlow criticized the $4 allotted for time and inconvenience. He said that the Center for Auto Safety did a survey and found it took two hours to get three estimates. Also to be figured in, he said, is time off from work to go to the repair shop and the consumption of gasoline when getting estimates and repairs.

Better Bumpers

Automakers could easily put better bumpers on their cars if they tried. Want proof? In testing 1991 models, the IIHS found that the 1991 Pontiac Grand Am sustained $1,146 in damage in a rear (into pole) crash test at 5 mph. However, a less expensive General Motors car—the 1991 Chevrolet Cavalier—suffered only $125 in damage in the same test. So the institute put the Cavalier bumper on the Grand Am and tested it again. *Voilà!* They were able to reduce the amount of damage by $600.

Look for Substance over Style

Until higher bumper standards are returned, be on the lookout when buying a car. Make yourself aware of styling decisions that weaken bumpers or prevent them from operating effectively.

Avoid cars that have lights, license plate holders, or exhaust pipes that are built into the bumper itself. The IIHS study in which cars were brought to drive-in claim centers found that damage to front bumpers was accompanied by damage to front lamps 72 percent of the time, and damage to rear bumpers meant damage to rear lamps 40 percent of the time. The study laid the blame on lamps, particularly front lamps, being part of bumper systems rather than being protected by them.

Also, look for hydraulic energy absorbers and steel or aluminum bumper reinforcement bars, which work better than fiberglass and plastic bars. For example, General Motors put out three similar 1994 passenger vans—the Oldsmobile Silhouette, Chevrolet Lumina, and Pontiac Trans Sport SE. The Silhouette had hydraulic shock absorbers, which compress and rebound to absorb crash energy, whereas the two others had only polypropylene foam to absorb energy. Although even the Silhouette didn't do all that well in 5-mph crash tests, it did out-perform the others. In a front-into-barrier test, for example, it had $419 in damage versus $809 for the Lumina and $1,336 for the Trans Sport.

Bumpers should wrap around the car body and extend out far enough to absorb the crash energy before it's transferred to the body of the car.

Check for front- and rear-end components that require whole assemblies rather than component parts to be replaced if damaged.

When considering a new car, the bottom line is to ask the dealer for the federally mandated insurance disclosure statement. Under NHTSA's Insurance Cost Information regulation, dealers are required to make available to prospective purchasers information reflecting differences in insurance costs for different makes and models of passenger motor vehicles. The data is based on differences in damage susceptibility and crashworthiness.

If you buy a car in California, Hawaii, or New York State, pay attention to bumper disclosure statements required by law.

New York has the toughest law. There, window stickers are

Table 5.1

INSURANCE INSTITUTE FOR HIGHWAY SAFETY
1993 MODEL 5-MPH CRASH TEST RESULTS

	Front into Barrier	Rear into Barrier	Front-Angle Barrier	Rear into Pole
Dodge Spirit	$229	$ -0-	$ 360	$1,182
Honda Civic	351	-0-	829	916
Saturn SL2	649	96	804	609
Ford Taurus GL	436	274	411	1,608
Pontiac Grand Am SE	304	708	1,125	906
Nissan Altima GXE	457	468	1,011	1,336
Mazda 626	801	1,041	931	652
Mercury Sable GS	528	325	753	1,879
Toyota Camry LE	679	548	1,669	1,522

required to show the maximum speed at which front and rear bumpers can hit a fixed barrier or be hit with a pendulum—all without causing damage to the body and safety systems or enough damage to the bumper itself—to require replacement parts. The car is also required to pass a corner impact test of at least 60 percent of that maximum speed.

Both California and Hawaii require window stickers, too, but automakers are given a choice about the wording. The stickers can simply say that the bumper system conforms to current federal standards and indicate the current mph standard, or they can give the front and rear impact speeds the car can sustain without damaging the body and safety systems or having to replace bumper parts.

6

Government Gyp #1: No Qualifications for Mechanics

Only two states—Hawaii and Michigan—and two counties —Broward and Dade in Florida—require auto mechanics to pass competency tests and to be certified. Elsewhere, a person without any training can work as an auto mechanic on your car.

It seems ludicrous for states not to have strict requirements for auto repairers, whose level of competency will impact auto safety, when they require all sorts of other professionals to be trained, tested, and licensed.

For example, in order to cut hair in Pennsylvania, a person is required to complete either 1,250 hours of schooling or 2,000 hours of apprenticeship and then pass a test.

To prepare taxes in Oregon, a tax preparer must obtain a license that requires completion of at least 80 hours of schooling and 780 hours of on-the-job experience, besides passing a test to show an understanding of theory and practice.

In order to sell real estate in Minnesota, it's necessary to complete 90 hours of instruction, pass a test, and complete an average of 15 hours of continuing education a year.

In Louisiana, a person who repairs radios (including car radios), TVs, citizens band radios, playback and recording devices, videocassette recorders, and satellite signal receiving equipment must pass an initial test, serve two years as an apprentice or spend two years at an accredited school, and then pass another test.

To be sure, testing and certification are required for auto mechanics who do state safety and emissions inspections. Also, air-conditioning service mechanics who handle chlorofluorocarbons, methyl chloroform, or carbon tetrachloride are required by the Clean Air Act to be certified. However, John Francis Foran, former chairman of the California Senate Committee on Transportation, couldn't understand why smog-check technicians are tested and certified while body shop mechanics are not. "Most people don't die immediately from an overdose of air pollution, but they can in a poorly repaired vehicle," he said.

ASE Voluntary Certification

To ward off state certification of auto mechanics, the auto industry in the 1970s set up the National Institute for Automotive Service Excellence (ASE) to run a voluntary certification program. ASE, which is now self-supporting, gives written tests in eight basic areas of the car: engine, automatic transmission/transaxle, manual drivetrain and axles, suspension and steering, brakes, electrical systems, heating and air-conditioning, and engine performance. There is also a test for those who do emissions-related diagnostics and repair—known as advanced engine performance specialists. In addition, there are tests for, among other things, collision repairers (see chapter 11).

As of spring 1994, ASE had certified some 342,967 technicians, with 70,483 master automobile technicians certified in all eight basic test areas. Another 35,004 collision repair technicians were certified, including 2,559 master body and paint technicians. Certification is good for five years.

ASE, however, has several flaws. It doesn't *decertify* for incompetence or fraudulent activities. "There's no real enforcement if someone goes amok," says Fred Pirochta, director of the Repair Facility Division of the Michigan Bureau of Automotive Regulation. Then, too, ASE doesn't publish lists of where to find certified mechanics. Also, whereas shops with ASE-certified mechanics can display a sign advertising that fact, there's no guarantee any of the mechanics will be certified in the area of the car the consumer wants repaired.

Finally, there doesn't seem to be any evidence that ASE-certified mechanics do any better repair work or are more honest than noncertified mechanics.

Reader's Digest, reporting in 1987 on a 33-state undercover survey involving 225 shops, said it got gypped in half the shops that promoted having ASE-certified mechanics.

Washington Consumers' Checkbook found in 1994 that only 71 percent of new-car dealers and non-new-car dealers employing at least one ASE mechanic were rated adequate or superior for doing work properly, compared with 75 percent of dealers *without* ASE-certified mechanics. With nondealers, the figures were 87 and 95 percent, respectively. Nevertheless, the magazine was still convinced that "the ASE program is a well-conceived, well-managed effort" and that "it is a good idea to ask that work on your car be done by a certified mechanic." The magazine still cautioned that the mechanic should be certified in the specialty area needed to fix a certain car.

Using ASE for Certification

The easiest way for states, cities, and counties to get into the mechanic certification business is to require that the ASE test be passed before a mechanic can work in a particular area of the car. This is what Florida's Broward and Dade counties did when they began licensing in the early 1990s. Michigan and Hawaii, which have been licensing mechanics since the 1970s, also accept ASE certification, although Michigan has its own tests as well.

Michigan began the licensing process by requiring all persons to pass the tests by a certain date. Hawaii, on the other hand, grandfathered in those who had worked as mechanics for at least two years before January 1, 1976, and registered with the state by June 30, 1976. Dade and Broward counties gave those mechanics practicing there on a particular date two years to become certified, while all newcomers after that date had to be certified in order to work in the counties.

These two states and two Florida counties allow trainees to work under the direction of certified mechanics. Besides certifying in the eight major areas, the two Florida counties also certify body shop mechanics. Michigan certifies those who do structural repairs on unibody vehicles.

Hawaii and Michigan have been certifying for life. To ensure that mechanics are up-to-date with the latest technology, the Michigan Bureau of Automotive Regulation has proposed three areas for five-year recertification: electronics and electronic systems, engine tune-up and performance, and brakes and braking systems. Broward and Dade require recertification every five years.

All four jurisdictions have their certification programs overseen by consumer protection agencies.

Rationale for Certification

There is a great need to attract talented people to the auto repair industry, and certification, apprenticeship programs, and mandatory training may be the only way to do it.

In 1992, according to *Intune with AC-Delco*, the average technician on the job was six to eight years behind in training. Moreover, only 20 percent of the nation's 5 million mechanics were fully trained to work on high-tech cars; the country was short an estimated 60,000 qualified mechanics, with the number growing by 2 percent a year.

Even many technicians who think they know their stuff are

in need of more training. Bill Sauer, president of AutoTech, a mechanic training school in Roseville, Minnesota, surveyed mechanics at more than 500 shops over a two-year period and issued a report in 1991. Whereas most mechanics gave themselves scores of 8 or 9 on a scale of 10 for competency in repairing modern computer-controlled cars, questions on theory cast doubt about their opinions. Only 4 percent knew the maximum allowable voltage drop across an electrical connection, and only 18 percent knew the purpose of an EGR valve or how an oxygen sensor works. (EGR valves had been around for 20 years, while an oxygen sensor is the heart of the computer system.)

Repairing today's cars, with their sophisticated electronics and unibody construction, requires that a mechanic have good reading, math, and logic skills. Whereas a high school technical education in auto repair might have sufficed years ago, William Arendt, chief of the Division of Vehicle Safety in New York state, says that these days high school programs cannot keep up with changing technology or provide training in basic systems. On the other hand, he says, "community college programs in New York are terrific," with graduates able to earn top dollar.

7

Government Gyp #2: Nobody's Watching the Crooks

Auto repair has constantly ranked at or near the top of consumer complaints for decades, yet few states or communities have done much to bring the industry under control.

Licensing and regulation of shops, with the power to put them out of business, is a reality in only six states—California, Connecticut, Florida, Hawaii, Michigan, and New York; four cities—Chicago, Dallas, Minneapolis, and Washington, DC; and four counties—Broward and Dade in Florida and Montgomery and Prince George's in Maryland. Body shops are licensed and regulated in an additional five states—Massachusetts, Nevada, New Jersey, Rhode Island, and Utah.

Half of the states don't even have so-called truth-in-auto-repair or disclosure laws or regulations. These usually address the customer's rights to obtain a written estimate, to be notified if the estimate is to be exceeded, to have replaced parts returned, and to get itemized repair bills stating whether parts installed were used, rebuilt, or reconditioned. States with these requirements, in addition to the six mentioned above, are Alaska, Colorado, Idaho, Indiana (the estimate is valid only for repairs over $750), Iowa, Maine, Maryland, Massachusetts, Minnesota, Montana, Nevada, New Hampshire, New Jersey, Ohio, Pennsylvania, Utah, Virginia, Washington, and Wisconsin. Tennessee law deals only with return of parts.

In addition, only body shops are required to make such disclosures in Oregon, and only new-car dealers are affected in Louisiana.

Additional provisions in some jurisdictions include giving customers a copy of any document requiring their signature immediately after they sign it (to prevent shops from adding unauthorized work to repair orders); giving an estimated cost of a teardown and reassembly whenever it's necessary to disassemble a system before an estimate can be given; and the spelling out of prohibited practices. Some locales have unique requirements: Montgomery County, Maryland, requires shops to put symptoms on the repair order; Chicago obliges shops to warrant parts and labor for 90 days or 3,000 miles unless disclaimed on the estimate and invoice; New York State requires shops to provide quality repairs; Broward County, Florida, demands minimum equipment for different types of repairs.

Provisions in some state laws are very tough. Whereas most states allow consumers to waive written estimates or not be entitled to them unless the repair is expected to reach a certain dollar amount, California requires a written estimate at all times. Likewise, the estimate cannot be exceeded without further authorization. Also, whereas most states require motorists to ask for their old parts back at the time their repair order is taken, Michigan and Maryland mandate return of nonwarranted parts. (In Michigan, parts that are heavy, oversized, or have a core value need be made available only for inspection.) This allows consumers and investigators to have evidence if parts were replaced unnecessarily.

Licensing Works

The experiences of California and Michigan show that licensing does work without costing the taxpayers a cent—the regulators are financed from license fees and penalties.

In the 1992–93 fiscal year, the California Bureau of Automotive Repair, a licensing authority, took 15,179 disciplinary actions; the vast majority were violation letters telling shop owners to change specific practices.

In the fiscal year ending June 1993, the bureau received 42,687 consumer complaints and was able to mediate $6,129,853 worth of refunds, rework, or adjustments even though the bureau isn't empowered to order restitution.

The bureau, which also oversees private garage emissions and lamp and brake inspections, works closely with the state attorney general and district attorneys, providing them with undercover cars to test the honesty of suspect shops. The cars are put into perfect shape with the exception of documented defects. They are then trailered within close range of the target shops and driven in by investigators. After repairs are made, the cars are trailered back to a laboratory where unnecessary or fraudulent repairs can be documented.

Whereas such undercover cars are considered essential to nabbing auto repair crooks and in deterring shops from trying to rip off customers, few state or local law enforcement agencies use them.

Meanwhile, while many states had major problems with Sears in 1992, Michigan didn't. Fred Pirochta, director of the Repair Facility Division of the Bureau of Automotive Regulation, believes it's because after more than 17 years of licensing and regulation, the message is out that allegations will be pursued. He says that the bureau jumped early on one Sears location for pushing unneeded repairs, then took swift administrative action, getting an assurance of discontinuance and restitution to consumers.

8

Safety and Emissions Inspections: The Private Garage Rip-off

In 1993, the Massachusetts Environmental Strike Force found that 64 of 135 private garage inspectors it checked deliberately altered the car or testing machine in an effort to help drivers pass the state emissions test. In addition, 85 percent of the garages failed to notice that the catalytic converter had been illegally removed.

In 1990, the U.S. Environmental Protection Agency (EPA) took vehicles that were preset to fail emissions tests to 75 repair shops in four states. The results: Two-thirds of the vehicles passed the inspection.

A woman in Maryland bought a used car, which is subject to a safety inspection in her state, and took it to three inspection stations. The first wanted to do $507.25 in repairs, including new front rotors, rear brake pads, a new horn, and a steering-box adjustment. The second shop said all those parts were fine but found $650 worth of other work to do, including new front brake hoses. The third shop said the brake hoses were fine but found $900 of other repairs to be done.

Such results call into question so-called decentralized safety and emission inspection systems, in which repair shops do both the inspecting and the repairs. Critics contend that such shops often either force unneeded repairs on motorists, go easy on regular customers, or just slap on inspection stickers—sometimes charging inflated prices without actually inspecting the car. In addition, the used-car inspections show too much is often left to the judgment of the inspector.

Currently, 21 states and the District of Columbia require annual safety inspections. Of those, only Delaware, the District of Columbia, and New Jersey have "centralized" test-only inspection stations. (New Jersey also has private garage inspection stations.) Some other states require safety inspections for vehicles changing ownership, automobiles that are new to the state, or rebuilt cars.

To implement the Clean Air Act amendments of 1990, the EPA required some 98 cities in 26 states with moderate smog and/or carbon monoxide problems to have "basic" emissions inspection and maintenance (I/M) programs in place by 1994. In addition, 82 cities in 22 states plus the District of Columbia are required to have "enhanced" I/M programs in place by 1995. The latter involve actual driving conditions simulated on a dynamometer at a variety of speeds and throttle settings.

Whereas "basic" inspections can be either decentralized (done by repair shops) or centralized (done by test-only stations), the EPA requires "enhanced" inspections to be done by test-only stations because of the bad results from private garage inspections. (California was given a waiver that allows repair shop inspections of two- and four-year-old cars.) Inspections are required to be biennial, although some states are doing "basic" inspections annually. Most states are using private companies to build and run test-only inspection stations. In the future, only three states—California, North Carolina, and Utah—are expected to allow the same repair shops to do both "basic" inspections and repairs. Another three states—Alaska, Florida, and Michigan—are expected to use a combination of decentralized and test-only stations. Future programs in Missouri, now with test and repair stations, and Ohio, with a hybrid system, are not yet finalized.

Although the auto repair industry has fought to keep private garage emissions inspections and to expand such safety inspections, their worth in improving safety or reducing emissions is questionable.

David Hemenway, an economist with the Harvard School of Public Health, maintains that under a decentralized system, "a kind of Gresham's law seems to operate, with lenient inspection stations driving out the strict ones." He contends that motorists, especially those with older, poorly maintained cars, "vote with their wheels" by searching for lenient inspection stations.

To test his theory, Mr. Hemenway examined the computer records of thousands of inspections done in Massachusetts in 1986. He found that inspection stations with the highest volume reported the fewest safety failures and had significantly lower emissions failure rates than other stations. They also tended to inspect a higher percentage of older cars.

"The typical motorist seems to prefer a quick, superficial, and passing inspection," he concluded.

The Annapolis *Capital,* after reviewing state police documents, concluded in 1989 that Maryland's decentralized safety inspection program was "plagued by slipshod car inspections, corruption, and consumer rip-offs." Some inspectors, it said, "pass cars that are too dangerous to drive, while others profit by 'fixing' nonexistent defects."

The newspaper found that nearly all the inspection stations that had repeated violations of state regulations were still doing inspections.

One problem in many states is that legislators won't allow safety inspection stations to charge enough money to cover the labor costs of the inspection. In South Carolina, for example, as recently as 1993 shops could charge only $3 for inspections, with 50 cents going to the state.

CENTRALIZED INSPECTION SYSTEMS

Are so-called "centralized" inspection systems any better? Here either a government bureaucracy or private company licensed by the government does inspections in assembly-line fashion and then sends you off to the shop of your choice if repairs are needed.

However, this system has its problems, too. For safety inspections, it's often inconvenient, requiring long drives for some people, and frequently creating long waiting lines. Both safety and emissions centralized testing may also require motorists to return after repairs and go through another inspection. There are some critics who argue that maybe all these inspections—both safety and emissions—should be scrapped altogether.

Pros and Cons of Safety Inspections

In the not-too-distant past, it was thought that safety-related periodic motor vehicle inspections (PMVIs) were part of the answer to reducing the highway death and injury toll. It even looked as if every state would have them. Under the National Traffic and Motor Vehicle Safety Act of 1966, the U.S. Department of Transportation (DOT) promulgated safety inspection standards. States had to follow these standards or risk losing federal highway construction funds.

In response to the threat, 11 states adopted periodic safety inspection between 1967 and 1972, bringing the total to 31 states. However, under the Highway Safety Act of 1976, Congress withdrew DOT's authority to withhold highway funds. As a result, between 1976 and 1982, 10 states repealed their inspection programs, including three states that had programs in effect before 1966.

Critics argue that there is no proof that PMVIs are cost-effective in reducing traffic accidents, and maintain that the money could be spent better elsewhere—perhaps getting drunk drivers and speeders off the road. (In 1993, 44 percent of fatalities were alcohol-related. And, according to DOT, one-third of all fatal crashes are related to speed.)

One of the problems in refuting these arguments is coming up with accurate statistics on accidents caused by defects in cars. Such data often come from police accident reports, but New York State officials point out that police officers are not mechanics and that their main concern at an accident scene is to take care of the injured and clear the area of hazards.

Nevertheless, a study done by the National Highway Traffic Safety Administration (NHTSA) for a 1989 report found that four inspection states had a 17 percent lower total accident rate than six noninspection states. Although the NHTSA adjusted its data to show no significant difference between inspection and noninspection states, a 1990 U.S. General Accounting Office (GAO) report did not agree with the adjustment and concluded that NHTSA should resume its support of state periodic inspection programs.

The big push for safety inspections comes not so much from safety advocates but from the repair industry itself, which sees them as a bonanza. The Motor and Equipment Manufacturers Association figures an additional $43 billion worth of safety-related components could be sold if all states required safety inspections.

There are some proponents of periodic inspection who think that it could be made more effective by having a centralized uniform national inspection and using tests for identifying defect rates among various cars.

At present, the various inspection programs are uneven. "In Maryland, a safety inspection takes 60 to 75 minutes," said the *Washington Post* in 1991. "In Virginia, it takes 20 minutes. In the District [of Columbia], three to five." Furthermore, said the paper, "about 40 percent of vehicles inspected in the District fail. The figure is 50 percent in Maryland, 35 percent in Virginia."

Data from a uniform test could be used to tell which safety components have high or low failure rates on various cars. This information in turn could be used for getting automakers to recall cars or extend warranties and to steer new- and used-car buyers to the safer cars.

Already, emissions inspections have identified which automakers have failure-prone emissions systems. For example, an analysis of vehicles under five years old inspected for the 1992 National Car Care Month found that General Motors cars failed emissions tests significantly more often than other models. GM vehicles failed the tests 14 percent of the time, compared to only 3 percent for Chrysler models and 7 percent for Ford vehicles and imports.

Emissions-Test Controversy

The EPA-mandated emissions inspection programs are also controversial. There are critics who claim that there is an alternative to running every vehicle through pollution-check stations and that the program will be a disaster because of, among other things, a lack of competent mechanics.

Donald Stedman, a chemistry professor at the University of Denver, argues against using inspection stations to find polluting cars. He's developed a remote sensing device for catching polluting vehicles as they go by on the road. It's an infrared spectroscopy device linked to a videocamera, which instantly records the carbon monoxide and hydrocarbon emissions from each passing vehicle as well as its license plate number.

However, Eugene Tierney, chief of EPA's I/M section, says such devices "fail cars that are clean and pass cars that are dirty." He does see a day, however, when roadside monitors may be used in connection with on-board diagnostic equipment and transponders (devices that emit a signal upon receiving an incoming signal) to catch polluting cars.

California set up a pilot project in late 1994 in the Sacramento area using remote sensors. Local car owners whose vehicles failed had to take a regular test or face a $250 fine.

Other critics are sounding warning bells about problems to come with EPA's enhanced I/M program. They cite a lack of technicians trained in high-tech emissions repairs and the inability of repair shops to afford enhanced test equipment (it costs over $100,000) necessary to determine if the repairs are effective.

In response, the EPA is helping states set up training programs to enable emissions mechanics to pass certification tests.

EPA rules also call for state oversight agencies to set up a hot line to assist technicians with specific repair problems and to regularly inform shops about common problems in particular engines. To steer consumers to the better shops, EPA rules require "report cards" be given to consumers getting enhanced tests. The reports must show, among other things, the percentage of vehicles from each shop that pass an inspection after repairs.

In addition, Tierney believes that shops can confirm the effectiveness of their repairs with $30,000 in equipment and, in fact, do not need to reproduce the test to make correct repairs.

Avoiding Rip-offs

To avoid inspection rip-offs at private garages, have things you know need repair fixed beforehand. That way, you may be able to get better-quality repairs at a better price than the inspection station offers. *Washington Consumers' Checkbook* found in 1994 that shops that do government-authorized safety or emissions work scored 9 percent lower than other shops in doing work properly. They also charged slightly higher prices.

9

The Emissions Warranty: Are You Paying for Free Repairs?

Dealers and other repair shops could be charging you for repairs that should be covered free under federally mandated emissions warranties. Some dealers may even be charging for repairs and then submitting warranty claims to the manufacturer.

Ending with the 1994 model year, the warranty for cars and light-duty trucks is 5 years/50,000 miles, whichever is first, covering performance (emissions tests) and design and defects.

The performance warranty covers any repairs needed to pass a state-mandated emissions test during the first 2 years/ 24,000 miles and any parts installed for the primary purpose of controlling vehicle emissions needed to pass a state emissions test during the next 3 years/26,000 miles.

The so-called primary parts include these systems: exhaust gas conversion, exhaust gas recirculation, evaporative emissions control, positive crankcase ventilation, air injection, early fuel evaporative, fuel monitoring, and ignition, along with hoses, gaskets, brackets, clamps, and other accessories. Among the parts included are the catalytic converter, oxygen sensor, EGR valve, PCV valve, air pump, thermal vacuum switch, electronic control module, electronic choke, and electronic spark advance.

The design and defect warranty covers parts that significantly affect emissions but whose purpose is other than emissions control —if their failure causes the car's emissions to exceed federal standards. Included in this category are the carburetor, choke, fuel-injection system, turbocharger, intake manifold, exhaust manifold, distributor, ignition wires, coil, and spark plugs. However, parts that have a stated replacement interval are warranted only up to the first replacement point.

Beginning with 1995 models, the performance and design and defect warranties have been cut back to 2 years/24,000 miles, with three exceptions: the catalytic converter, the electronic-emissions-control unit (including some 39 parts), and the on-board emissions diagnostic device (plus associated parts such as hoses, switches, sensors, solenoids, gaskets, seals, wires, harnesses, and connectors). The exceptions carry an 8-year/80,000-mile warranty.

The manufacturer can deny warranty coverage to drivers who fail to follow its maintenance schedule for the particular system that failed, or whose vehicles show evidence of tampering, abuse, or use of improper fuels (i.e., using leaded fuel in a vehicle that takes unleaded). Maintenance can be done by the driver or any repair shop, and while drivers are free to use any brand of parts, these must be of equal quality to the original ones. It's wise to keep receipts.

You must get the warranty work done at a dealership of the manufacturer of your car. All parts, labor, diagnosis, and miscellaneous items are free. If you are ever denied coverage, ask for a complete reason in writing and the names of those involved in the denial as well as the name of the person you should contact to appeal the denial. Once you've exhausted the manufacturer's procedures for filing a warranty claim, you can write for help to: Warranty Complaint, Field Operations and Support Division (6406J), U.S. Environmental Protection Agency, Washington, DC 20460.

It may be best to get your emissions test from some place other than the dealer, who might pass you to avoid warranty repairs.

For further information, the EPA offers two free booklets from the above address: *What You Should Know About Your Auto Emissions Warranty* and *If Your Car Just Failed an Emission Test . . . You May Be Entitled to Free Repairs*. (For related information, see *Get Your Car Fixed Free*, published in 1994 by Consumer Reports Books.)

10

Never Give a Sucker an Honest Brake Job

Don't fall for low-cost brake specials. They're basically a come-on to sell you high-priced repairs you may not need. During the early 1990s, Sears used its own hook to get customers into the shop: ads offering a $59.99 front disc-brake special along with a free brake inspection.

"The price advertised at 'low cost' outlets is not what you end up paying," warns Allied-Signal Inc., maker of Bendix brake products. "Any subsequent work the shop performs—replacing hardware, front wheel seals, repacking/replacing wheel bearings, inspecting or replacing brake hoses, servicing other brake components—will be added on as additional charges."

The results of a reader survey published by *Consumer Reports* in September 1994 (see chapter 32) found that the median price for a brake job performed between January 1990 and March 1993 was $150 at private garages, $180 at chains, and $200 at dealers. Nearly 30 percent of *Consumer Reports* readers who took their car to a chain for brake work were responding to an ad, and 28 percent of these chain customers complained of misleading prices in the ads.

You'll know for sure you're being misled if the ad or commercial mentions that the special doesn't apply to semi-metallic brake pads, which most cars use.

Generally, for front disc brakes the come-on ads offer to install new brake pads, turn and true the rotors, install new oil seals, repack the wheel bearings, inspect the calipers, and do a road test.

Not included is the flushing and refilling of the brake fluid and the possibility the rear drum or disc brakes will also need the same sort of service. There's also the possibility that an expensive complete brake system overhaul will be needed, including the replacement of such components as calipers, rotors, pistons, and wheel cylinders.

Fred Pirochta, director of the Repair Facility Division of the Michigan Bureau of Automotive Regulation, worries that brake repair customers are routinely sold calipers and rotors, and he's not sure it's necessary. However, he said, manufacturers have had to replace asbestos in pads and linings with other friction material, and that could be causing more wear problems, noise, and damage to rotors.

James Sepulveda, deputy district attorney of Contra Costa County, California, says there's no way of knowing whether a shop that says the calipers need to be replaced is telling the truth "unless you really know something about brake calipers and how they work." Otherwise, he says, you wouldn't know what questions to ask.

He says that the best defense if a shop wants to replace your brake calipers is to get a second opinion. At the second shop, "don't tell them what the first shop said." Also, he says, after repairs, get your old parts back in case you need to prove they were replaced unnecessarily.

Sepulveda says there is a way, however, to prevent being sold unnecessary brake pads. He recommends asking the shop about the amount of wear on the pads and the manufacturer's specifications for wear. You can then look in your owner's manual to see if they're telling the truth about the manufacturer's wear tolerances.

There also appears to be widespread overselling of master cylinders, which hold the brake system's hydraulic fluid, pump it to the wheels, and activate the calipers and wheel cylinders. A 1989 undercover operation by the Nassau County, New York, district attorney's office found five shops that tried to sell investigators unnecessary master cylinders.

Also, watch out for shops that want to replace your rotors or drums instead of resurfacing them. Again, ask for the manufacturer's tolerances. You can avoid ruining your rotors and drums by replacing brake pads before they entirely wear out.

Allied Signal says that the following three symptoms, while possibly indicating brakes in need of repair, could also involve simple solutions:

- *The car pulls to one side when the brakes are applied.* This could be caused by an underinflated tire or misadjusted brakes.
- *Brakes grab with the least pressure on the pedal.* This could be linings contaminated by grease or oil.
- *The brake pedal nearly touches the floorboard before brakes function.* You may just need a simple adjustment.

What type of shop is best for brake repairs? The *Consumer Reports* reader survey found that consumers were most satisfied with the work of independents.

11

Body Shop Insurance Repairs: Are You Being Cheated?

Robert Juniper, Jr., spends over $200,000 annually on editorial-like advertising for his huge Three-C Body Shop in Columbus, Ohio. His one overriding populist message: Auto insurance companies, which provide him with 87 percent of his work, are shortchanging the public when it comes to repairs.

Juniper particularly dislikes the insurance industry practice of directing claimants to so-called "preferred provider" shops that will do repairs for their price—often meaning at a discount. He maintains that it's difficult to do quality repairs at what the insurance companies offer. He also says insurers often want to install nonoriginal equipment crash parts (see chapter 12), which he maintains "don't fit right and rust faster."

More or less agreeing is Donald A. Randall, former Washington counsel of the Automotive Service Association (ASA), the country's largest trade group of auto repair shop operators. He says insurance-paid body repairs "are often not quality repairs. They are frequently substandard and mediocre" and vehicles are often "not restored to their precrash values."

Randall, who spearheaded a U.S. Senate investigation into the auto repair industry in the 1960s, figures consumers are losing more than $4.5 billion annually for less than fully restored vehicles. That figure is based on the assumption that at least half of the 45 million vehicles involved each year in an accident will not receive $200 each worth of needed repairs. The problem, he says, is that there's no independent check to ensure that safety and emissions systems have been properly restored.

"The average vehicle owner," says Randall, "does not possess the expertise to judge whether the vehicle has been correctly restored, and most owners merely inspect the paint finish and interior, and accept the more important mechanical and structural repairs with little or no scrutiny."

Indeed, of 52 damage-repaired cars from the Sacramento area and Orange County, California, selected at random from insurance company claim files, only 29 percent had been repaired properly and 40 percent evidenced fraud, according to a 1994 report by the state's Bureau of Automotive Repair. The report said poor workmanship and fraud adds $866 to the average repair bill. Similarly, a couple of years earlier, WSB-TV in Atlanta had experts go over seven damage-repaired vehicles paid for by insurance. Only one of them was judged a first-rate repair and five had structural problems ranging from mild to severe. In addition, a van had paint that didn't match, and the welds on one vehicle had not been finished off properly—a factor that could cause rust.

Whereas insurers say that directing customers to their preferred shops saves consumers time and money and ensures quality repairs, it must often be done subtly because many states, including Ohio, outlaw the practice as anticompetitive. However, in Massachusetts, under a 1988 law insurers may require a customer to select a repair shop out of a list of at least five shops in their geographical area. In return, the insurer must guarantee the quality of the materials and workmanship, and the shop must complete the repairs without undue delay for the amount offered by the insurer, plus any deductible. Insurers said that a regulation under the law requiring them to give only a short list of preferred shops cut everyone's insurance premiums by $30 to $40 a year. However, a new regulation in 1994 forced insurers to list not only their preferred providers but all licensed shops in the county.

Body Shop Fraud

Fraud among body shops is believed to be rampant. Moreover, defrauding insurance companies on accident repair claims has developed into a major problem. New Jersey insurance commissioner Samuel F. Fortunato estimates that body shop repair schemes cost insurance companies in that state as much as $240 million a year, boosting premiums for every policyholder in New Jersey by $60 a year.

New Jersey has perhaps the most aggressive insurance fraud unit in the country. In one of many investigations, an undercover agent posing as an appraiser received 48 bribes from 17 auto body shops between 1990 and 1992, according to the state attorney general's office. The bribes, totaling $5,655, added 28 percent to bills, or $45,209, officials said. Bills were reportedly inflated by adding hours of labor never performed or parts not replaced.

In 1992, undercover police in the San Fernando Valley of California posed as sellers of stolen auto parts. They made some 75 arrests at body shops and dismantled yards that bought their goods. Agents from the Florida insurance department set up a fictitious adjusting company and alleged in 1992 that body shop operators offered bribes to inflate insurance payments by some $10,000. In Tennessee, state officials in the early 1990s broke up a price-fixing conspiracy among body shops. A new-car dealer and body shop, both in Memphis, paid penalties of $100,000 and $70,000, respectively.

DON'T GET CLIPPED

One of the more insidious insurance company and body shop practices is "clipping" or "sectioning" one car to another.

A man in Florida had expected the repair of the wrecked rear of his new 1984 Chevrolet Cavalier to be covered by his insurance, including new parts. He went to see the progress of the repair work at a Sarasota, Florida, dealership and was shocked at what he found. The dealer had welded the back of another car onto the front of his car. The man sued on grounds that he had not been informed that his car was going to be clipped, as well as fraud, voiding his warranty, devaluation of his car, and odometer discrepancy (the rear end had five times as many miles on it as the front end). He settled out of court during a jury trial.

This man was lucky. Usually people never find out about their car being clipped, or if they do, it's not until they're in a minor accident and the two halves of the car separate.

John W. Grow, former chief of the California Bureau of Automotive Repair, says that "in the event of a violent collision . . . [a clipped car] will not manage energy [crush] as well as the original. Occupant injury can be expected to be more serious. A technician of less than journeyman level can produce not only an inherently dangerous car but a troublesome and valueless car as well."

Beware of Paint Specials

Low-cost paint specials may not be the bargain you think they are. The job may look sloppy, with runs and thin spots. Often the vehicle is not sanded or primed before the new paint is applied. That could result in the paint peeling or chipping within a relatively short time. All too often, that low-cost paint special may be just a come-on to sell you higher-priced repairs.

It Pays to Shop Around

In 1990, *Bay Area Consumers' Checkbook* found a substantial difference in quality among body shops in the San Francisco area. Twenty shops were rated "adequate" or "superior" by 95 percent or more of their surveyed customers for doing work properly, while 13 shops were rated "inferior" by 30 percent of their customers.

The magazine, in a survey of its subscribers and those of *Consumer Reports*, also found independent body shops had a higher average score than dealers for doing work properly— 89 percent versus 70 percent.

Unibody Repairs

Cars made with frames began to be phased out in the late 1970s. Most modern cars are now made of "unibody" construction, in which supports and sheet-metal body parts are spot-welded together in a single unit. This makes it easier and cheaper to assemble cars and offers greater crash protection to occupants. Instead of the force of a crash being localized at the impact point, it is spread throughout the vehicle.

The main disadvantage of unibody construction is increased damage to the vehicle in areas remote from the impact. It also takes highly specialized knowledge and proper equipment to repair structural damage to unibody cars. Your best protection when getting unibody repairs is to make sure the shop has mechanics trained by the Inter-industry Conference on Auto Collision Repair (I-CAR) and certified in structural analysis and damage repair by the National Institute for Automotive Service Excellence (ASE).

I-CAR is a nonprofit training organization specializing in auto body repair. It offers several different types of courses, including a 32-hour collision repair course. Look for I-CAR "gold-class professionals"—collision repair shops in which 80 percent of the staff are I-CAR trained—or call 1-800-ICAR-USA to find the nearest shop.

ASE also gives certification for collision repair painting and refinishing, nonstructural analysis and damage repair, and mechanical and electrical components. I-CAR and ASE have been jointly developing other tests.

Unfortunately, a survey by the California Bureau of Automotive Repair released in 1994 found that only 12 percent of body shops had even one I-CAR trained person. Also, many shops didn't have proper equipment—half didn't even have the right devices for returning vehicles back to their original shape.

Assorted Tips

When dealing with body shops and insurance companies, keep these tips in mind:

- *Choose body shops that belong to trade organizations.* They're more likely to keep up with the latest techniques, and you may be able to get help from the organization if something goes wrong. Two prominent national organizations are the Automotive Service Association and the Society of Collision Repair Specialists. There are also many state and regional trade organizations, such as the California Auto Body Association and the Washington Metropolitan Auto Body Association.
- *Don't urge shops to save the deductible or deal with a shop that offers to save the deductible.* If they're willing to cheat the insurance company, they're probably also willing to cheat you.

  New Jersey officials, for example, came across a case where an appraiser had authorized new parts for a car. The car's owner then told the repair shop to install used parts so he could cover the $500 deductible. The insurance company paid $3,333 for the repair job, all based on new parts. However, the shop shortchanged the customer by not installing $600 worth of parts, new or used. The car owner and the shop owner were each fined $1,500 and had to make restitution to the insurer.

  Saving the deductible is becoming more of a problem because consumers attempt to keep down insurance costs by raising their deductibles.

- *Before accepting the vehicle, compare the estimate with the final invoice to make sure they match.* Levin Barnes of South Carolina didn't do a comparison and paid the bill. Later, he compared the two and found he was shortchanged $968.68 for parts not installed and labor not performed as per the $3,762.28 estimate. He then had to sue to recover the amount.[2]

- *Don't rent a car from a dealer body shop.* This might discourage the shop from doing repairs quickly, since the longer it takes, the more rental money it makes.

- *Be on the lookout for "Bondo bandits."* These are shops that charge for pounding out a dent or replacing a crash part, but instead fill the dents with body putty. Go over the body of your car with a magnet. If the magnet doesn't stick to what should be metal, you have probably discovered a "Bondo bandit" and should contact the district attorney's office.

- *Don't settle for incomplete repairs.* Look over your car and make sure that new and old paint colors match, chrome is free of paint, doors and windows close easily and tightly, doors and panels are evenly gapped, surfaces are smooth and show no evidence of sanding or grinding, moldings and paint stripes align, and body panels have no bumps or waves. Try to take delivery of your car in bright sunshine so you can properly inspect the paint job; then take the car for a test drive before signing any release.

- *Don't accept an incomplete invoice.* Make sure that all parts and labor are itemized and any used parts and nonauto manufacturer parts are clearly identified.

- *You don't always have to hassle with the other person's insurance company.* Under motor vehicle financial responsibility acts, a few states, such as Iowa and Nebraska, provide a surefire way to get someone who damages your car in an accident to pay up. If you win in small-claims court and the other party doesn't pay, the state will take away the person's driver's license and vehicle registration until payment is made.

12

The Crash Parts Controversy

Are crash parts (fenders, hoods, doors, etc.) made by independent producers in Southeast Asia—and derogatorily referred to as "Taiwan tin"—a blessing or a curse for consumers?

On the one hand, producers from the Far East have broken the monopoly auto manufacturers had on crash parts for their cars and have brought down prices. On the other hand, critics say the parts are not as good as the automakers' crash parts, may not fit as well, and rust more easily.

This debate is highly important to you if an insurance company is paying for your crash repairs. When alternative crash parts are available, insurance companies will often insist that car owners choose them over so-called original equipment manufacturer (OEM) ones because they're cheaper. Crash parts are about a $9-billion-a-year business, and according to Ford Motor Company, the insurance industry influences 75 percent of all purchases. The insurance companies say that crash parts competition saves them about $400 million a year.

Monopoly Buster

Before alternative crash parts became available in the late 1970s and 1980s, the auto companies were able to raise prices at will. For example, between 1970 and 1979, according to the Western Insurance Information Service, crash-parts prices increased 318 percent, whereas new car prices went up by 63 percent and the overall cost of living increased by 106 percent.

Since that time, however, crash-parts prices have dropped where there has been competition and continued to rise dramatically where monopolies have been maintained. For example, between 1983 and 1987, when competition arose, a Dodge Aries fender dropped from $221 to $87 and a Chevrolet Chevette fender from $129 to $71, according to the Insurance Information Institute. Meanwhile, where there was no competition, the cost of a Chevrolet Caprice front door rose 151 percent from $267 to $671, the institute said.

Prices also dropped steeply for many crash parts in the early 1990s as a result of competition. Ford dropped prices on its competitive body parts an average of 14 percent. In 1991, a fender for a 1985 Chevrolet Camaro was reduced in price by about 20 percent—from $207 to $167—because of a competitive fender costing $142.

Quality Questioned

Are these copycat parts as good as the originals? Are insurance companies gypping you by insisting they be used in repairs (or you must pay the difference)?

In 1992, Ford won $1.8 million from Keystone Automotive Industries Inc., the nation's largest distributor of aftermarket crash parts, in a federal court suit over false advertising claims. As part of the ruling, Keystone took out corrective ads admitting, among other things, that its crash parts didn't meet Ford's manufacturing specifications for fit, finish, weight, and overall quality, and that its parts might corrode at a faster rate than Ford crash parts.

The California Auto Body Association maintains that consumers are hurt by non-OEM parts. They say body shops have to keep cars an average of three days longer to get the parts to fit properly. The organization also says the warranties and rust protection may not be as good. In the end, said the association, non-OEM parts could reduce a car's resale value.

The Automobile Protection Association (APA), a Montreal-based consumer group, agrees that non-OEM parts generally have not been as high-quality as OEM parts. In a study released in 1990, it found that while the influx of non-OEM parts has reduced insurance industry costs, the savings may be coming out of the pockets of either body shop operators, who must spend additional unpaid time to install and finish the parts, or consumers themselves, "who may obtain a lower-quality repair." The APA also said that warranty protection for non-OEM parts "falls far short of that offered by some OEMs." Non-OEM warranties, APA added, apply to the replacement part, "but not to its installation or finishing," whereas some OEM warranties cover all three.

The report advised owners of late-model cars to insist on OEM parts or imitation parts approved by the independent Certified Automotive Parts Association (CAPA). You can write to CAPA (see Appendix) for a list of certified parts, or look for a yellow oval sticker on crash parts bearing the word CAPA. In 1994, only about 13 percent of generic crash parts were CAPA-certified.

Nevertheless, be aware that some critics contend that even CAPA-approved parts may not meet OEM standards. Kenneth Myers, marketing manager for Ford's parts and service division, announced at the national Autobody Congress and Exposition in 1990 that there were "gross deficiencies" in CAPA-certified parts. He said a certified Ford Escort fender took 10 minutes longer to install, a CAPA-certified truck hood had half as many welds as the original, and none of the CAPA-certified parts Ford tested used galvanized steel to provide corrosion protection.

Karen Fierst, deputy executive director of CAPA, says Ford was "not forthcoming" with information to back up Myers's claims. She says that since 1989, CAPA has required certified parts to undergo costly electrodeposition painting (EDP) for rust protection and upgraded its standards in 1992 to provide for better fit and quality.

Laws and Regulations

Most states require the insurer and/or body shop to disclose when non-OEM parts are to be used. Some states, however, go further.

In Indiana, insurance companies must give you a choice between new OEM, new non-OEM, or used crash parts during the first five years after the model year of the vehicle. In Wyoming, insurers can't directly or indirectly require the use of non-OEM parts, and they can't authorize any repair or accept any estimate using non-OEM parts unless the consumer consents to it in writing. Texas prohibits insurance companies from specifying the brand name or type of crash part. Oregon requires insurers, without the consent of vehicle owners, to use only those non-OEM parts that are certified by an independent test facility as being equivalent in quality to the part being replaced in respect to fit, finish, function, and corrosion resistance. They must also warrant such parts. New Hampshire requires insurers to use only those non-OEM parts that are at least equal to the original parts in fit, quality, and performance.

Patented Fenders?

The auto manufacturers are trying to get a federal law passed allowing them to patent their crash parts and to hold exclusive rights for 10 years. The Big Three once had more than

90 percent of the crash-parts market for their cars and now have about 65 percent.

If a design patent law ever passes, critics say crash parts prices and auto insurance costs would rise dramatically.

As it is now, some monopoly crash parts such as doors and hoods often retail for more than clothes dryers and refrigerators, which are far more complicated pieces of machinery and subject to much competition.

The automakers justify the high costs of monopoly crash parts by pointing out that they must supply replacements for parts where there is little demand, while outside suppliers sell only fast-turnover parts.

CRASH PARTS AND TOTALING

The higher that auto manufacturers can keep crash-parts prices, the more cars they can sell. This is because there is a direct correlation between an insurance company's decision to declare a car a total loss, forcing the owner to buy another car, and parts prices.

A study by the Alliance of American Insurers found that it would cost $62,700 to replace all the parts on a new 1993 Ford Taurus with a sticker price of $19,095.

Thus, a decision to total the car would be based on the $62,700, not the $19,095. Theoretically, damage to only 10 percent of the Ford Taurus could produce a repair bill for parts and material alone of $6,270. In such a scenario, even moderate damage can make a car not worth repairing, especially if it is three or four years old.

13

The Service Contract Scam

Automobile service contracts, which insure key components after the original warranty expires, are an estimated $5-billion-a-year business. About half of all new-car buyers as well as many used-car buyers purchase these contracts, according to the Federal Trade Commission.

How could so many people be so wrong?

Auto service contracts, on average, return only a few cents on the dollar, and, according to the New York State attorney general's office, are subject to "rampant price gouging" by dealers who sell them. In addition, car owners might also be paying for protection that they would normally get for free under the manufacturer's warranty (or are entitled to get for free under state implied-warranty laws).

Additionally, many firms in the business have gone bankrupt, or their owners made off with the reserves, leaving customers in the lurch. Most states don't safeguard consumers by regulating such contracts as insurance.

If all this isn't enough to discourage you, consider that many service contracts may not provide you with protection you thought you had. Also, some contract providers might put you through the wringer before paying off claims—if they ever do.

Typically, service contracts cover the power train—engine, transmission, differential, and driveshaft. A few may cover other parts as well and may include extras such as towing, road service, rental cars, and meals and lodging if a trip is interrupted. Most service contracts have a deductible—usually one for each repair visit.

Whereas many people have gotten back more than they paid for such contracts, the odds are very much against it.

Just what a bad deal service contracts represent can be seen in the lawsuit between Nissan Motor Corporation in U.S.A. and Adesco, Inc., which handled Nissan's service contracts. Court documents showed that Nissan dealers typically sold service contracts on 1984-87 model cars for $795, of which only $131 (16.5 percent) went to pay for repairs. The rest of the money went toward dealer profits ($555, or nearly 70 percent), Nissan's corporate profits ($60), Adesco's fee ($38), and a motor club ($11).

The Nissan-Adesco suit also showed that trucks had the lowest percentage of claims. While trucks accounted for 30 percent of all contracts sold, they represented only 14 percent of all claims. At the other extreme, turbocharged cars had the highest claims by percentage. The major problem for all cars was the electrical system, accounting for 37 percent of all claims.

A big reason that service contracts return such a low percentage of every dollar spent is dealer greed. Markups often start at 100 percent. A 1990 report from the New York State attorney general's office estimated that in 1989 consumers nationwide overpaid by $300 million for auto service contracts. This was based on a survey that found that in 1989 half of the

New York service contract buyers—175,000 people—paid more than the Big Three auto manufacturers' suggested retail prices or paid over double the Toyota dealers' costs. The average overcharge was more than $200.

In one case, a Chrysler dealer charged a customer $1,620 for a service contract that had a suggested retail price of $250 and had cost the dealer $125.

Often, dealers sell service contracts with high-pressure sales techniques, giving the car buyer no prior chance to study the manufacturer's warranty in order to spot duplication or fully read and understand the terms of the contract.

Unfortunately, only California and Washington State have cooling-off periods in which a customer can cancel an auto service contract and, provided there have been no claims, get a full refund. In California, notification must be made within 60 days for a new vehicle and within 30 days for a used vehicle; in Washington, within 30 days (a cancellation fee of up to $25 can be assessed after nine days). California also mandates a pro rata refund after the 60/30 days or within the 60/30 days if a claim has been made. In such cases, a fee can be charged not exceeding $25 or 10 percent of the price of the contract, whichever is less.

In several states, where implied warranties can't be disclaimed or modified, dealers may be engaging in deceptive trade practices by not disclosing to contract buyers that they are paying for protection already granted them for free. (See chapter 29 for details on implied warranties.)

Take the Money and Run

Another minus for service contracts is the fact that many warranty administrators—those who provide the contracts to dealers—as well as dealers themselves have gone bankrupt or have run away with their customers' money, leaving claimants with little or nothing. In the late 1980s and in 1990, at least 15 warranty administrators failed. In many cases, claimants never got a cent, or else received only a percentage on the dollar.

Sometimes contracts exclude so much that they're worthless. Exempt from coverage on many contracts are certain specified parts, damage caused by overheating not directly attributable to the failure of a lubricated internal part of the engine, consequential damages, and more.

Some contracts also may not pay up if a noncovered part causes a covered part to fail. Others might exclude or limit liability if you don't bring the car back regularly for maintenance —even if the maintenance has no relation to what went wrong.

Then, there are contracts that tell you only what they cover. Unless you're a mechanical expert, you won't be able to figure out what they don't cover.

Even if your contract says it covers what went wrong, you may have a hard time collecting. The Federal Trade Commission (FTC) in 1991 charged Griffin Systems, Inc., a Cleveland-based mail-order service contract firm, with not answering its phones and then not paying claims on the grounds that the consumer didn't get prior authorization for repairs. An FTC administrative law judge in 1993 ruled that Griffin engaged in "false, misleading, and deceptive" practices.

Warranty Administrators

While auto manufacturers are legally responsible for their service contracts and auto insurance companies are responsible for theirs (called "mechanical breakdown insurance"), contracts issued through warranty administrators and sold by dealers are less understood. Such contracts are legal between the dealer and the customer. If the dealer goes out of business or the customer moves out of town, the contract could become worthless. Also, whereas warranty administrators themselves are usually insured against the dealer going out of business (and even its own inability to pay claims), that so-called reinsurance is only as good as the insurance company backing it. Unfortunately, only about 20 states regulate vehicle service contracts as insurance, with all the safeguards that entails—including money in reserve (some of those states exclude automaker contracts). The only other safeguard is buying a contract backed by a top-quality insurance company. However, only a few of the top insurers are willing to engage in the vehicle service contract business.

Many dealers like to sell warranty administrator contracts because they can often make more money on the sale and the repairs.

What to Do

Consumer Reports advises you to save yourself a lot of expense and possibly grief by forgoing service contracts altogether and instead buying models that its reader surveys show hold up well over time (see the *Consumer Reports New Car Buying Guide*). According to the surveys' findings, new cars with a higher probability of problems are newly introduced models, cars with turbocharged engines, and four-wheel-drive vehicles.

You must also take into account that if anything major does go wrong after the manufacturer's warranty expires, there's a chance the auto company involved will still make a free repair (see chapter 22 on secret warranties) or be forced to make repairs if safety defects are involved.

Used-vehicle buyers, as an alternative to a service contract, might consider getting a clean bill of health for the vehicle from an unbiased diagnostic center (see chapter 19).

If you're a worrier, consider putting money regularly into an interest-bearing savings account so you'll have enough money to cover any repairs. Consider performing all the preventive maintenance suggested in your owner's manual, as that may be the key to avoiding breakdowns and abiding by the warranty.

If you do buy a service contract, mechanical-breakdown insurance is often the cheapest, since it's usually sold over the phone or through credit unions and thus cuts out dealer profits. You can get discounts on suggested retail prices for regular service contracts—if you shop around. For example, any GM dealer (not just the one where you bought your car) can sell you a service contract on a GM car.

There may be one advantage to buying a service contract: It could give you implied warranty rights under the Magnuson-Moss Warranty–Federal Trade Commission Improvement Act (see chapters 28 and 30).

14

Rustproofing and Other Rip-offs

Would you pay an auto dealer $200 to $400 or more for a product of dubious value that, according to the Council of Better Business Bureaus (CBBBs), usually costs the dealer less than $50?

Millions of car owners have.

The product is "aftermarket" rustproofing—so-called because it's applied after the vehicle is shipped from the factory.

Several studies and investigations lean toward the conclusion that you'd better hold on to your wallet on this one:

- In a 1989 study, the Society of Automotive Engineers

inspected 528 five- and six-year-old cars in Michigan and found rust perforation (rust that eats through the sheet metal) on less than 3 percent of them. "I don't believe aftermarket rustproofing is necessary," concluded the study's main author, Arthur W. Bryant, "especially with the present materials used by most automakers and the length of most rust-through warranties."

- In a 1990 report, the CBBB concluded that many people who buy aftermarket rustproofing probably don't need it.
- In 1989, the Maryland state attorney general's office ordered General Motors, Toyota, and Nissan dealers in the state to inform customers before trying to sell them aftermarket rustproofing that their respective manufacturers built additional corrosion resistance into their cars and considered such rustproofing unnecessary. Dealers were charging up to $1,000 for the service. The negative publicity caused aftermarket rustproofing in the Washington, D.C., metropolitan area to fall from 65 percent of new-car purchases to less than 20 percent.

Despite these negative reports, many dealers and independent aftermarket rustproofers contend that additional rustproofing is necessary wherever a large amount of salt is applied to winter roads; wherever coastal airborne saltwater can cause corrosion; and/or wherever acid rain or other "environmental fallout" is present. They also say that aftermarket warranties usually cover rust caused by road salt and environmental factors, whereas most manufacturer warranties do not.

Although aftermarket rustproofing's ability to combat salt and pollutants is debatable, there are plenty of other reasons for you to avoid this overly expensive add-on: the way it's applied, service warranties full of loopholes, deceptive sales practices, and the lack of consumer protection legislation.

The Application

Dealer-applied rustproofing could accelerate rather than retard rusting, since it's necessary to drill holes to reach hidden areas and it's therefore possible to clog draining ducts with rustproofing material. In addition, improperly applied rustproofing compound could adversely affect window regulators, seat belt retractors, door locks, propeller shafts, bumper energy-absorbing units, shock absorbers, and more.

There is an alternative method of applying rustproofing other than drilling holes. It's called the "fogging" method, which calls for a fine mist to be sprayed into the vehicle's body cavities through existing access holes. However, hole-drilling advocates contend that fogging doesn't ensure that the compound will be applied thoroughly and in the proper thickness.

Unfortunately, whatever the method, few consumers are expert enough to know if any particular dealer is applying rustproofing correctly and not causing more harm than good.

Perhaps even more confusing are rustproofing warranties. The CBBB study said none of the manufacturers warranties and very few of the aftermarket warranties cover surface rust. The rust must completely eat through the sheet metal to be covered.

The CBBB report also said "lifetime" warranties offered by aftermarket rustproofers do not always mean what the term implies. In fact, they usually limit the liability for repairs to the book value of the car. "If at any time the cost of a single repair, when added to the total cost of all previous repairs, exceeds the book value of the car at the time the repair is needed, the warranty will not cover the repair," the report said.

Then, too, says the report, many "lifetime" warranties require an annual or periodic inspection or cleaning, possibly involving a fee—sometimes at high dealer labor rates. If you miss an inspection, your warranty is invalidated.

Some aftermarket warranties contain the phrase "repair or refund." This may give the rustproofer an option to give you your money back rather than repair the more costly rust damage.

There are also aftermarket warranties that exclude untreated areas. This could mean that if the applier missed some spots and these rust through, you're not covered.

In addition, some aftermarket warranties won't pay as long as the manufacturer's rust warranty is in effect, or they limit the number of claims or become invalidated if you don't send in a registration form or complain immediately.

Furthermore, rustproofers may not have adequate insurance to cover all of their claims (only Wisconsin appears to require rustproofers to be insured). Rustproofing companies may also take an inordinate amount of time to accept or reject a claim, and they will often reject claims without giving a valid reason.

Then there are the dealers who try to sell customers on the idea that aftermarket rustproofing and the added warranty will enhance the value of the car when it is traded in or sold. The CBBB report contended that such assertions "can be overstated." It pointed out that the National Automobile Dealers Association's own used-car guides, which establish used-car values in many parts of the country, "list many options that add to or detract from the value of used cars." However, said the report, "they do not list after-manufacture rustproofing itself, or its lifetime warranty, as a value-added feature."

If you're concerned about premature rusting, frequently and thoroughly clean the areas of your car where road salt, mud, and other corrosive materials tend to accumulate.

Only a few states, such as New York, Ohio, and Wisconsin, have tough laws or regulations concerning the rustproofing business.

Paint Protection

Some dealers may try to sell you paint sealant, perhaps for anywhere from $200 to $600, which they claim will protect your car from pollutants such as acid rain. Don't believe it. A Ford spokeswoman told the *New York Times* (November 9, 1991) that the company had tested more than 100 commercial sealants and that none of them worked against acid rain. What's more, do-it-yourself paint-protection sprays and upholstery-protection sprays are available at auto parts stores for far less money.

15

Dealer Service

You might think that a dealer's service department would be the best place to get your car repaired. The mechanics at such facilities have access to special factory training and technical bulletins. They specialize in a narrow range of cars and should get to know them well. They are also among the highest-paid mechanics in the industry and are likely to have passed industry certification tests. They probably have state-of-the-art equipment as well.

In fact, consumers take a dim view of dealer service departments. In a 1994 report, *Washington Consumers' Checkbook* analyzed over 36,000 consumer ratings of auto repair shops in the Washington, DC, area. It found dealers about 15 percent less likely to satisfy customers and about 17 percent more expensive than independent shops. In surveying customers of 46 General Motors dealership service departments, the report found that the average GM dealer was rated by 33 percent of its customers as inadequate in doing work properly the first time.

Why is dealer service generally so bad? Part of the explanation may be that dealers tend to get the toughest repair jobs. There's also the corruption and carelessness stemming from the flat-rate pay system (see chapter 1), and the fact that mechanics and retail customers are forced to subsidize warranty repairs.

However, the main problem seems to be the use of commission-based service writers as a bridge—some might say a barrier—between customers and mechanics.

Instead of allowing customers to describe their vehicle's problems directly to the mechanic and perhaps have the mechanic probe for more information, customers are forced to give such descriptions to what are known as service writers. These are usually people in white smocks who are chosen for these jobs not because they're good mechanics but because they're personable and good salespersons.

Often the service writer will not communicate the customer's description of the problem but instead will make a diagnosis—often inexpert—and write on the repair order for the mechanic to do a particular repair or to check out several possible defects. The mechanic then does what the service writer instructs, which might have nothing to do with the actual problem.

Service writers are also usually paid a commission, which encourages them to run up the repair bill. Many dealers claim such commissions are necessary to light a fire under service writers so that they will give prompt attention to customers.

(In an effort to keep customers after the warranty expires, Ford Motor Company has begun franchising service-only dealers, where customers can talk directly to the mechanic.)

Dealer service is also often overly expensive. Many dealers price themselves out of the market by using a single labor rate.

"Shop Supplies"

One of the more devious dealer tricks is adding a phony percentage surcharge to bills, usually labeled as "miscellaneous shop supplies" or "shop materials." This is supposed to cover items that have no part number or are of too little value individually to list separately on an invoice. Examples are nuts, bolts, washers, lubricants, paper floor mats, and fuses.

James Muntz, editor of the newsletter *Warranty Dollars & Sense*, believes charges for materials are justified. He says that the average service manager or warranty administrator estimates shop supplies not charged on repair orders at between $8 and $12 per day per mechanic. However, dealers typically charge 5 to 10 percent of the total parts bill or total labor bill or both.

The District of Columbia specifically prohibits "shop supplies" or similar type charges, whereas Colorado specifically allows them. Such charges are also prohibited in Idaho, Iowa, Louisiana (dealers only), Minnesota, Montana, and Ohio, where repair shops must itemize all materials used. Laws in some other states requiring itemization of parts used, such as in California, also appear to preclude such charges.

Independent Businesses

Auto manufacturers advertise the services of their dealers and control many aspects of their business, but don't expect the automaker to come to your aid when you have a complaint against a dealer. When things go wrong, dealers suddenly become—in the eyes of the auto companies—independent businesses over which they have no control.

For example, when a man from Quebec Province had an accident with his new 1992 Topaz GS while vacationing in Florida, he took the car to a Lincoln-Mercury dealer. The dealer took 2½ months of the owner's four-month vacation to complete the repairs. He spent $712 renting a car for a month and couldn't afford to rent it any longer. He complained to Ford but got this typical response: "Each Ford dealership is privately owned and operated. Ford Motor Company cannot interfere in any dealership's policies and/or practices. Therefore, we feel that this matter must be resolved between you and the dealer." Eventually, through the intercession of *The Gazette* in Montreal, Ford sent the man a check for half the rental car fee.

DEALING WITH THE DEALER

While generally it's best to avoid doing business with new-car dealer service departments—especially large urban ones—this isn't always possible. Sometimes they're the best place for certain repairs, particularly those involving engines. So if you must deal with a dealer, look for one that is a member of the American Automobile Association's approved repair shop program (see chapter 25). In its 1994 report, *Washington Consumers' Checkbook* found that such dealers scored 6 percent better in customer satisfaction than dealers not in the program.

You should also attempt to speak <u>directly to the</u> mechanic who is to work on your car. If that's not possible, insist that the service writer write on your repair order the symptoms your car is experiencing and when they occur, but nothing else. Don't let the service writer put his or her diagnosis on the order, and certainly don't sign any repair order that has notations such as "check engine" or "check transmission." This tells the mechanic how to go about the diagnosis and increases the repair bill. Also, don't allow the service writer to put instructions on the repair order that involve fixing broad categories, such as "repair transmission" or "repair exhaust system." This could result in the unnecessary replacement of your transmission or exhaust system when minor repairs might solve the problem.

Resolving Complaints

If you have a complaint about a dealer service department, first take it up with the service manager. If you get no satisfaction, go to the general manager or owner of the dealership. If you still aren't satisfied, you might try to get the problem resolved through AUTOCAP, a dealer complaint-handling program (see Appendix). You might also complain to the agency in your state that licenses dealers or to the local or state consumer protection agency.

If you are charged an outrageous percentage fee for shop materials, you can sue in small-claims court and make the dealer justify the charges with an itemized list.

16

Muffler and
Exhaust Rip-offs

Be leery of lifetime warranties on mufflers.

A staffer at Consumers Union had the exhaust system on his Toyota Corolla replaced at a Midas Muffler and Brake Shop for $143.90 and received a lifetime warranty. Two years and three months later, according to *Consumer Reports* (August 1989), the muffler burned out and was duly replaced under warranty. However, there was a $152.44 charge for replacing the rest of the exhaust system—$8.54 more than the previous repair.

William Arendt, chief of vehicle safety services in New York State's Department of Motor Vehicles, says lifetime muffler warranties may be more beneficial to the shop than to you. He adds that such warranties assure the shop that it will continually get your exhaust system work, since there's a good chance you'll also need a tailpipe, catalytic converter, or other part along with the muffler.

Also be leery of low-cost muffler specials. The New York City Department of Consumer Affairs launched an investigation in 1989 against Meineke Discount Mufflers. It found that although the company advertised replacement and installation for between $18.93 and $26.95, consumers ended up paying an average of $99 for muffler repairs—with a range of $60.20 to $303.

Inspectors took cars with a two-inch hole punched in the side of their muffler to 20 Meineke franchised shops. Seventeen of the shops wanted to charge between $29.88 and $65 for the muffler alone, and 10 shops wanted to charge extra for clamps and labor.

Although the three other shops agreed to sell mufflers within the advertised price, they charged for pipes, clamps, labor, and sometimes unnecessary repairs, putting the totals between $45 and $151, according to the allegations.

Six shops wanted to perform unnecessary repairs ranging from $6 to replace hangers to $250 to replace a catalytic converter, the department said. Meineke agreed to pull the ads.

In a 1993 *Consumer Reports* reader survey on muffler repairs, those surveyed said that independent shops did the best job. Among the chains, Cole in three states and Car-X in the Midwest and FLorida were the highest ranked in overall satisfaction. (See chapter 32 for details.)

Catalytic Converters

A catalytic converter helps reduce smog by controlling exhaust emissions. When a shop sells you one, make sure it's a three-way and not a two-way. Three-way converters control emissions of hydrocarbons, carbon monoxide, and nitrogen oxides, whereas two-ways do not control nitrogen oxides.

In 1993, Cole Muffler, Inc., with 50 shops in New York,

Pennsylvania, and Florida, paid the largest penalty ever imposed by the Environmental Protection Agency for installing two-way converters (considered tampering with the installation of catalytic converters). The company paid a $238,000 penalty for some 3,288 violations. The agreement required Cole to replace, free of charge, each catalytic converter that was improperly installed.

For more information on what's legal, get the EPA pamphlet *Aftermarket Catalytic Converters*. The address is Field Operations and Support Division (6406J), U.S. Environmental Protection Agency, Washington, DC 20460.

17

Air-conditioning: Good-bye Freon, Hello Hassles

Most auto air conditioners will be obsolete by 1996 because an international treaty—the Montreal Protocol—mandates the phaseout of chlorofluorocarbons, which destroy the ozone layer. The production of CFC-12, better known by its Du Pont trade name of Freon, will be banned at the end of 1995, and only recycled and stockpiled CFCs will be available.

Auto companies have embraced an alternative, known as HFC-134a, which 1995 cars are equipped to handle (as are most 1994 cars and some 1993 cars). However, many older auto air conditioners will have to be significantly modified to use it.

Simon Oulouhojian, president of the Mobile Air Conditioning Society (MACS), expects that there will be more than 140 million vehicles in the United States equipped with CFC-12 air-conditioning systems by the time production ends. He estimates that a retrofit to an air conditioner in good working order will cost between $200 for newer cars (those built after 1990, which have nonporous hoses and the tighter seals required to handle HFC-134a) to $800 for older cars. However, he anticipates that "most retrofits will occur when a system fails," entailing higher costs.

Already, though, rip-offs in connection with the phaseout are appearing. Some people are being sold R-22 and other "claimed" drop-in replacement refrigerants to use in their car's air-conditioning system. Oulouhojian warns, however, that R-22 is not intended for automotive air-conditioning use and "can cause seals and hoses to deteriorate and increase system pressures, possibly rendering the system inoperative." Drop-in refrigerant blends may contain butane, isobutane, and propane, which could cause an explosion. There is also a worry that these substitutes could get into a shop's recycling system and cause damage to other customers' vehicles as well. They could also void the warranty on your air-conditioning system.

Then there's the leaky air conditioner scam. In Arizona, several shops told customers that they couldn't refill leaky air-conditioning units with Freon because the Clean Air Act prohibited them from knowingly releasing the refrigerant into the atmosphere. The mechanics then told customers they had two choices: pay up to $1,000 to have the leaky units overhauled or sweat out the summer.

However, the Arizona state attorney general's office issued a warning to shops in 1993 that this was a misinterpretation of the act, simply used as a pretext for performing unnecessary repairs. EPA literature states that leaky units may be refilled without first repairing the leaks. It should be noted that all auto air-conditioning systems leak refrigerant. As the system gets older and the seals and hoses deteriorate, the leaks get worse. After about four or five years, enough refrigerant has escaped to cause a noticeable loss in cooling performance. Most auto owners then bring the vehicle in to be recharged. (To reduce serious leaks, owners should periodically run the air conditioner —even in winter—to lubricate the compressor seals.)

Besides potential rip-offs, other air conditioner problems loom as well.

Oulouhojian is not sure who will do all the retrofit work. He says that in 1993 there were about 20,000 outlets specializing in air-conditioning and about 138,600 other shops that did air-conditioning service work. Even without retrofits, he cautions, some shops have their hands full during hot weather. He's also concerned that shop owners may be reluctant to invest in retrofit facilities and equipment, knowing that demand will probably drop off within five years. And he doesn't know whether enough technicians can be trained to do the work or whether HFC-134a components and parts will be readily available for the aftermarket, considering the heavy demand for components and parts for new-car production.

When buying a 1993 or 1994 model used car, be sure to check whether it uses HFC-134a. Otherwise, you might be in for an expensive retrofit repair sometime in the future.

For more information and a free booklet, *Auto Air Conditioners and the Ozone Layer: A Consumer Guide,* call the EPA's stratospheric ozone information hot line at 800-296-1996.

18

Jurassic Park Used Cars

Some used-car lots in America are potential Jurassic Parks where vehicles thought to be extinct—totaled by insurance companies and turned into scrap—are brought back to life and sold to unsuspecting consumers. Such lots may also hold someone else's new-car nightmare: a lemon bought back by the auto manufacturer and then sold—in many cases without being fixed and without telling the next purchaser of its sordid history.

A Jurassic Park used vehicle is exemplified in the case of Clarence Campbell. Less than a week after he bought a used 1979 Ford F-100 pickup, the accelerator linkage stuck against the firewall. This caused the truck to accelerate uncontrollably, jump a curb, and strike three pedestrians in Mobile, Alabama, killing one of them and injuring another. Unknown to Campbell, he had bought a salvaged vehicle that had changed hands many times.

His Ford had been bought new in late 1979 by Gary Nicholson, who wrecked it the following year by running into the rear end of a flatbed trailer truck. Among other things, the front end was badly damaged and the engine was driven back into the firewall.

Nicholson's insurer, Dairyland Insurance Company, totaled the car and took ownership. It then sold the car to a salvage dealer, Late Model Auto Parts. Although the insurer was required by Alabama state law to forward the vehicle's title, manufacturer's identification number plate, and license plate within 72 hours to the Department of Revenue, it didn't do so.

Late Model then sold the car to L. R. Boyette, who had a body shop repair the truck. However, the shop didn't do any work on the firewall. Boyette occasionally had trouble with the accelerator sticking but was able to free it by tapping the accelerator pedal. After a few months, he sold the truck to Rudolph Phillips, who gave the truck to Treadwell Ford as a trade-in.

Treadwell then sold the truck to Campbell. Treadwell had performed an inspection but didn't look at the firewall, where a defect caused the fatal accident.

A court found Treadwell responsible for the accident because it did an inadequate inspection and engaged in misrepresentation. It also found Dairyland partially at fault, but in 1986 the Alabama Supreme Court overturned that part of the decision.

The Supreme Court said that the law the insurer violated was intended to prevent motor vehicle theft and not to avoid motor vehicle accidents. Furthermore, the court said, Dairyland had nothing to do with the repair work, nor did it sell or attempt to sell the truck to anyone other than the junkyard for salvage.[3]

As this case illustrates, salvage, titling, and disclosure laws are so weak that buying a used car in most states is akin to playing Russian roulette. Not only could that gleaming beauty in the used-car lot have been in a crash, a fire, or a flood, but it could even be two cars—the good front end of a car hit in the rear, welded to the good rear end of a car hit in the front. When two-cars-in-one are involved in accidents, the two halves could come apart and eject the occupants.

The National Auto Auction Association estimates that the sale of rebuilt salvage cars without disclosing their history cheats consumers and used-car dealers alike out of up to $4 billion annually. Indeed, an estimated 6 million vehicles on the road in 1993 were wrecked in collisions and then rebuilt and sold, often to unsuspecting dealers or consumers.

Whereas nearly all states require rebuilt cars to be inspected by a state official, for the most part (as in the Alabama case) the purpose of the inspection is to look for stolen parts and to prevent transfers of license plates from wrecks to stolen vehicles.

In only a few states does a state official inspect rebuilt vehicles for safety and structural integrity before allowing them to be sold. Perhaps the most thorough of those states is Utah. There, an official trained by the Inter-industry Conference on Auto Collision Repair (I-CAR) inspects vehicles three times during the rebuilding process—once before any work is done, another time after welds are made, and once again when the job is completed. However, only vehicles up to seven years old are inspected.

Several other states require rebuilt cars or cars entering the state to undergo a state safety inspection. But critics say such inspections—usually done by private garages—are subject to corruption (see chapter 8), and few inspectors are skilled in judging the structural integrity of vehicles.

Further complicating matters is that only Michigan and Dade and Broward counties in Florida require mechanics who rebuild cars to pass a competency test in structural analysis and damage repair. Hawaii, however, requires shops that restore salvaged vehicles to post a $25,000 bond, which can be forfeited if a shop willfully departs from or disregards accepted practices of workmanship. The shop also has to rebuild vehicles to automaker specifications and allowable tolerances.

Another problem is that few states make insurance companies responsible for preventing badly damaged cars from ever being rebuilt. Rhode Island solves this shortcoming by requiring insurance companies to divide total-loss vehicles into two classifications of salvage—those that can be used for "parts only" and those that are considered repairable. However, vehicles that individuals salvage are not classified.

Compounding the lack of state vigilance in ensuring that salvaged vehicles never get back on the road again or are rebuilt to some sort of quality standard is the laxity of many state vehicle titling laws. As of mid-1994, three states—Alaska, Washington, and Wyoming—didn't require the titles of wrecked vehicles to be branded as "salvage," according to Richard Morse of the National Highway Safety Traffic Administration (NHTSA). This allows operators in other states to "wash" titles by sending wrecked or rebuilt cars to those states and getting "clean" titles, which give no indication that the cars were ever salvaged.

Some other states are also used to washing titles because they allow certain repaired wrecks to get clean titles. Kentucky, for example, has been a haven for washing titles because clean titles can be obtained if repairs are done for under 75 percent of the car's value. Rebuilders often get around this law by using cheap parts, cheap labor, used parts, or all three. Some 30,000 salvaged vehicles received clean titles in Kentucky in 1992, according to the state's Motor Vehicle Commission.

Several states, however, do require the titles of repaired wrecks to be branded for life.

Another problem is that of disclosure. Although many states require sellers of used cars to disclose former salvage cars, in practice this is often not done—either out of deception or because used-car dealers themselves were fooled. However, dealers have access to computerized title-tracking services, which should greatly cut down their chances of being fooled.

To combat the problem, a U.S. Department of Transportation task force was set up under the federal Anti–Car Theft Act of 1992 to recommend uniform state standards for dealing with salvaged vehicles and to implement a computer bank by 1996 that would allow state motor vehicle administrators instant access to vehicle histories in all 50 states.

Mr. Morse of NHTSA, who chairs the task force, said that his organization has proposed legislation forbidding cars with damage exceeding 75 percent of their book value from being rebuilt and returned to the road without passing a special state inspection conducted by those trained in unibody and frame construction.

Also proposed were three uniform titles: (1) "salvage," when first wrecked (available only within 15 days for vehicles with damage exceeding 75 percent or more of their book value); (2) "rebuilt salvage," if a car passes a stringent safety inspection; and (3) "nonrepairable," if a car can't be safely rebuilt. Additionally proposed was that once safely rebuilt, a vehicle would have a metal decal saying "rebuilt salvage" riveted into the front doorjam.

Until all these consumer protection measures are in effect, Morse's advice is to have a used car inspected by a mechanic before you buy. "It takes five minutes for a good mechanic to tell you it's been wrecked," he said.

Palming off New-Car Lemons

A 1992 investigation by the *Hartford Courant* tracked four new-car lemons bought back by the manufacturer and resold by an auto sales auctioneer in Connecticut. Whereas the auction properly notified dealers who bought the repurchased lemons, only one of the next four purchasers was told by the dealers that the car was a lemon. The three not informed, who lived in Massachusetts and New York, said they wouldn't have bought the cars if they had known their histories.

One of the three purchasers bought a 1988 Oldsmobile for $8,500 and returned it to the dealer six times for repairs. In fact, the car still had the same problems that resulted in its being returned to the manufacturer in the first place.

Palming off lemons bought back from disgruntled customers without disclosing their histories appears to be a widespread practice among auto manufacturers. In 1993, General Motors Corporation and 34 GM dealers in the San Francisco, Sacramento, and Fresno areas were accused by the California Department of Motor Vehicles of not revealing lemon buybacks as required by state law. GM paid a $330,000 penalty, with its dealers paying $750,543. Also in 1993, GM paid $95,000 in penalties and restitution in Washington State for selling 11 lemon buyback vehicles through auction to dealers, who sold the cars without the required disclosure or without revealing that they carried a mandatory 12-month/12,000-mile warranty. In both cases, GM denied that it violated the law. In 1988, Chrysler Corporation agreed to pay up to $2 million to those who bought 392 cars in New York State that were not disclosed as lemon buybacks as mandated by state law.

About 20 states don't even require subsequent purchasers to be notified that they are buying a lemon. This allows the automakers to dump lemon buybacks from elsewhere in those states. Even many of the states that do require disclosure exclude lemons that are bought back before arbitration or a court suit.

There are still other shortcomings of lemon buybacks:

- Only four state lemon laws require the manufacturer to actually fix the problem that resulted in the buyback before it can resell the vehicle. They are Hawaii, South Carolina, Texas (if the buyback was ordered by the Texas Motor Vehicle Commission), and West Virginia. In addition, Georgia, Vermont, and Washington State require serious defects to be fixed, and Minnesota and Pennsylvania prohibit returned vehicles from being resold at all if they had a complete failure of the braking or steering system likely to cause death or serious injury.
- Only some 11 states require disclosure of the specific defect that resulted in the buyback.
- Less than a fifth of the states require manufacturers to warrant lemon buybacks for 12 months or 12,000 miles.

Equally scandalous is that only a handful of states require titles to be stamped as former lemons so that all subsequent buyers know they're getting one.

(For ways to avoid purchasing a lemon buyback or salvaged vehicle as well as other used-car buying tips, see chapter 19 or *Consumer Reports Used Car Buying Guide*.)

19

How to Avoid Used-Car Repair Nightmares

You'll have to be on your toes in most states to buy a used car that won't give you repair headaches.

In 1978, the Federal Trade Commission (FTC) proposed that used-car dealers inspect cars before selling them, disclose certain major defects and estimate their repair costs, list previous owners and known repairs, and disclose if the vehicle had been declared a total loss by an insurance company. This was later watered down by the FTC to just requiring that dealers disclose known defects among 52 possible major defects. Congress, facing a well-financed used-car lobby, vetoed that regulation in

1982. In 1983, the U.S. Supreme Court ruled that such vetoes were unconstitutional and so the agency tried again.

In 1984, the FTC issued its present Used Motor Vehicle Trade Regulation Rule. This simply requires dealers to fill in and post a limited-information "buyer's guide" window sticker. Dealers must check off whether the vehicle is sold either "as is—no warranty" or "warranty." The "as is" portion warns that "the dealer assumes no responsibility for any repairs regardless of any oral statements about the vehicle." The warranty has a checkoff for a full warranty or limited warranty and space for the dealer to provide the percentage of parts and labor it will pay for, the systems covered, and the duration of the warranty.

Despite the leniency of this rule and the threat of a $10,000 fine, many used-car dealers are not using the stickers or are not following guidelines. Illinois officials in 1992 made a surprise inspection of 78 used-car dealers and found 51 percent of the 2,374 cars examined did not have an FTC window sticker.

Most of the states have also failed to protect consumers from defective used cars. Only a handful of states mandate used-car warranties or disclosure of defects.

Connecticut, Massachusetts, Minnesota, and New York require cars meeting certain age, mileage, and cost restrictions to carry mandatory warranties. Minimum warranties are also required in Illinois if there is no "as is" disclaimer in the contract, and in Rhode Island if the warranty is not disclaimed in writing.

Used-car lemon laws, including arbitration provisions, are in effect in Massachusetts, New York, and Rhode Island. Dealers in those states have three tries or anywhere from 10 business days to 30 days to fix defects during the warranty period or return the purchase price. Maine requires warranted cars to be fixed within five calendar days, excluding Saturdays, Sundays, and holidays—and within 35 days if parts are unavailable.

Maine, Pennsylvania, Wisconsin, and the District of Columbia require all or certain known defects to be disclosed.

Several states do not allow used-car dealers to modify or disclaim the implied warranty of merchantability, giving consumers in those states protection for vehicles sold without warranties or with expired written warranties (see chapter 28).

The New York Model

Of all the states, perhaps New York offers the best protection for used-car buyers. First, dealers are required to inspect and correct 18 safety items to certain specifications and then to certify that the vehicle "is in condition and repair to render, under normal use, satisfactory and adequate service upon the public highways at the time of delivery."

Next, dealers must give warranties for used cars that were sold or leased for over $1,500. If the vehicle has 36,000 miles or less, the warranty must be for 60 days or 3,000 miles, whichever comes first; if it has more than 36,000 miles but no more than 100,000 miles, the warranty must be for 30 days or 1,000 miles. Covered parts must include the engine, transmission, drive axle, brakes, radiator, steering, alternator or generator, starter, and ignition system (excluding the battery).

If a defect substantially impairs the value of the vehicle and the vehicle has been out of service for a total of 15 days (45 days if parts are unavailable) or the dealer has made three unsuccessful tries to fix the same defect, all during the warranty period, the dealer must accept the return of the vehicle and refund the full purchase price or lease payments.

A mandatory 30-day warranty should solve most used-car defect problems. In an analysis of used-car complaints received in 1982, the New York City Department of Consumer Affairs found that 23.2 percent of defects surfaced the first day, 46.3 percent within the first week, and 81.8 percent within the first 30 days.

Rules of Engagement

Consumers are not on an even playing field when buying a used car. The seller likely knows what's wrong with the car, but isn't likely to tell a buyer. Here's how to level that playing field:

- *Have the vehicle independently inspected.* The cost is minimal compared with what a defective car might cost you. If possible, take the car to a diagnostic center or diagnostic van run by an American Automobile

Association (AAA) affiliate—or to any diagnostic center that doesn't do repairs. About 14 AAA clubs have diagnostic centers or vans. For example, the California State Automobile Association, covering Northern California and Nevada, has eight diagnostic centers open to anyone. It charged members $40 to $56 in 1994, with nonmembers paying more. Diagnostic vans, available to members only, visit local AAA offices. The cost is $38.

As an alternative, you might pay a mechanic to inspect your car. Two franchised organizations that offer this service are Auto Critic of America, based in Dallas, and Car Checkers of America, based in Bridgewater, New Jersey.

- *Pay for a title search.* This will help you avoid a car that was salvaged, has a rolled-back odometer, or was a new-car lemon bought back by the manufacturer. If the vehicle has never left your state, your motor vehicle department may be able to conduct the search. Otherwise, Carfax, Inc., in Fairfax, Virginia (800-274-2277), might be able to do it.
- *Check the reputation of the dealer.* For complaint records, contact your Better Business Bureau, local consumer organizations, and the agency in your state that licenses used-car dealers.
- *Look for the FTC sticker or any state-mandated sticker.* Don't do business with any dealer that doesn't supply them.
- *Keep an eye out for odometer tampering.* Don't buy a car that doesn't come with a completed odometer statement. Federal regulations require that the statement give the odometer reading. It must also certify that, to the best of the seller's knowledge, the odometer reading reflects the actual miles that the vehicle has been driven or that the reading cannot be relied upon. Warning signs of odometer rollbacks include excessive wear of the brake pedal or floor mats, tampering with the dashboard, and contradictions in the mileage levels recorded on oil-change stickers. Every rollback of 1,000 miles is said to add about $50 to the price of a

car and makes it more likely the car will need repairs sooner than you had anticipated.

- *Check the title before you finance.* People who finance a used car often don't see the title until they've paid off the loan, since the title goes to the finance company. It's only then that they discover the title has a salvage or lemon buyback designation.
- *Get maintenance records.* Get evidence that a car has been properly maintained and an idea of which parts have been replaced. This is especially important if you buy a car within the emissions warranty period and need proof of proper care.
- *Avoid split warranties, where the dealer offers to pay a percentage of the repair costs.* "Repairs under split warranties are invariably inflated by dealers to the point where the consumer ends up paying for the total cost of repairs," says the New York State attorney general's office.
- *Watch out for "curbstoners" when buying from an individual.* "Curbstoners" pretend to be selling a privately owned car—often doing the deal in the street—but they are really dealing cars without a license or are connected with a licensed dealer. They often sell high-mileage cars bought at auctions with the odometers rolled back, as well as fixed-up wrecks, flood-damaged cars, and stolen vehicles. Curbstoners use classified ads, For Sale signs in car windows, and swap meets. One alleged swindler in San Diego bought wrecks, took them across the Mexican border to Tijuana for repair, and then sold them to local college students. He hid the fact that the cars had "salvage" written on the titles by doing all the paperwork himself.

    To avoid curbstoners, make sure you know where the seller lives, do your own transfer paperwork, and be suspicious if the name on the car title is different from that of the person selling the car.
- *Read up on which are the best used cars and which to avoid.* The April issue of *Consumer Reports* gives a Frequency-of-Repair chart, based on reader experience,

for each car model going back eight years. Also consult the *Consumer Reports Used Car Buying Guide.*

- *Watch out for rental cars going by another name.* The automakers buy back cars from rental car companies and then auction them off to their dealers. However, not all dealers like to call them rental cars. Instead, they refer to them as "program cars," "factory officials," "factory executives," "factory auction cars," "special factory cars," "nearly new cars," or "fleet repurchases."
- *Check for safety recall.* Find out if the car you're considering has been subject to a recall and has been fixed. First, call the NHTSA hotline (800-424-9393). Have ready the vehicle identification number (VIN), make, and model of the car. If there has been a recall, ask a dealer for that manufacturer or its district service office (see the owner's manual) to check whether the particular car you are considering was checked for the defect and, if necessary, repaired.
- *Take a magnet with you.* Go over the body of the car with a magnet to find sheet metal that has been filled with putty instead of straightened out or replaced.
- *Check closely for flood-damaged cars.* Here are a few tips from auto auctioneers ADT Automotive, Inc., for sniffing out flood-damaged cars: Pull up the trunk mat and feel for dried residue or silt. Look for anything that looks painted in the undercarriage, then check for a water line inside door panels and the trunk area. Look for rusty or painted door screws, seat tracks, and lug nuts.

  "The biggest problem is silt remaining after a car is dried out," says Ron Hope, national service director for ADT. "This fine, abrasive powder is impossible to completely remove from a vehicle. It gets in the crevices, and over time becomes a conductor of electricity and causes failures in the electrical system or wears down the brakes at a much faster rate than should be expected."
- *Don't buy at night.* Look the car over in daylight so that you can see body defects. Choose a dry day so you can look for fluid leaks on the ground.
- *Take it through a car wash.* This is a good way to see if there are any leaks.

20

Highway Robbery: Hoodwinks away from Home

Many auto repair rip-off artists ply their trade at gas stations that target vehicles with out-of-state license plates. They're usually located adjacent to interstate highway interchanges with heavy vacation travel.

"Many times people don't know they've been victimized," says Rick Beseler, chief investigator for the state attorney's office in Jacksonville, Florida. These criminals count on the fact that if their victims do realize they've been cheated, it won't be until they're back home or far away. By then, they won't want to return and testify against the crooks in court.

Reader's Digest, in a 1987 nationwide undercover probe, found that stations along interstates liked to take "$20 or $30 bites" for such unneeded items as fuel filters and oil additives, or for spark plug cleanings that are never done.

Station attendants typically do their tricks when you stop for fuel or to use their rest rooms. Here's what you might encounter while you're not looking, according to Beseler:

Smoking alternator. Attendants will carry in their front pocket a small eyedrop bottle filled with antifreeze. They'll spray it on the hot alternator, causing it to smoke, then sell you a new alternator. But what they actually do is paint your old alternator with a quick-drying silver paint.

Pinning a radiator. Attendants will conceal a pinner—a small screwdriver filed down to resemble an ice pick—in the palm of their hand and stick it into the radiator or a radiator hose, causing water and steam to come out. They'll then sell you a new radiator or hose. A variation on this scam is to push down on the radiator hose, causing a gush of water to come out that, says Beseler, "looks like Old Faithful." You'll be charged for a new radiator, but the mechanic will merely do a simple soldering job.

Pinning a tire. A pinner is also used to puncture a tire so you'll buy a new one. Also to sell new tires, attendants will point to little bumps on your radial tires' sidewalls and say that your tires are separating. Actually, such bumps are normal.

Slash and sell. Attendants will cut or put holes in belts and hoses and sell you new ones.

Here are some additional scams attendants have used:

Water pump. Attendants will loosen the main nut on your water pump, making it leak badly. They'll then charge you for a new water pump but will actually just tighten the nut.

Shock absorber leak. Attendants will squirt oil onto one of the shock absorbers while you're not looking and will then point out to you that it's leaking. They'll then try to sell you two new shock absorbers.

"Salting" the alternator. Attendants will distribute metal filings around the alternator and then tell you it means the part should be replaced. Usually, they'll just paint your old alternator and charge you for a new one.

Exploding battery. Attendants will plop Alka-Selzer tablets into the battery cells and replace the caps. Soon, an explosion occurs, blowing off the caps and creating smoke. You're then sold a new battery.

Spark plug wire. Attendants will loosen a spark plug wire, causing the engine to miss, then charge you for new spark plugs. Often, they'll just clean the old ones.

Fuel pump drip. Attendants will spray an oil-and-gas mixture on the fuel pump, point to the mixture dripping on the ground, and sell you a new fuel pump.

"Short-sticking." Attendants will offer to check your oil, but will push the dipstick down only far enough so that it registers a quart low. Or else they will stick it in all the way but wipe off part of the oil and claim it shows you are a quart low.

Gas cap caper. Attendants will steal your gas cap, tell you that yours is missing, and sell you a new one.

Some shops will sabotage your car not only to sell you unneeded repairs, but also to get you to pay for expensive long-distance towing or to get you to stay in a motel they just happen to own while you're waiting for your car to be fixed.

PROTECTING YOURSELF

To avoid such away-from-home rip-offs, stay with your car while an attendant is checking it. Be suspicious if your vehicle was fine when you drove it into the service station and suddenly developed a problem there. Insist that you get your old parts back and that the invoice includes the name, address, and telephone number of the service station; that it itemizes parts and labor; and that it notes whether parts are new, used, or rebuilt.

Tips When Traveling

One way to minimize the chance of being ripped off while traveling away from home is to join the American Automobile Association (AAA) and have your car repaired at one of its approved repair shops (see chapter 25) or a shop that performs towing for the organization. The AAA may be able to help get your money back if things go wrong. You could also invest in an AAA Plus membership, which gives 100 miles of free towing and costs $15 to $25 extra. On the road, you can call AAA's super number: 800-AAA-HELP. Even if no approved repair shops are around, the local club may know of good facilities that can repair your car.

An example of what can happen to you is told by a man in Tulsa, Oklahoma, in a letter to the *St. Petersburg Times*. He alleged that a franchised repair shop totally fouled up the brakes on his Winnebago motor home during a 1990 trip to Florida. He said that the shop charged him $746.56 for a brake job, including rebuilt calipers (including pistons), new disc pads, two new rotors, and a rebuilt master cylinder. After traveling on, he had to pay more to have part of the work corrected —the calipers had been installed upside down and on the wrong wheels, Ford pistons had been put in Chrysler calipers, and the rear brake shoes were not making contact with the drum. When he got back to Tulsa, he had a complete brake job done for $504.03. The shop in Florida refused to make restitution. He consulted attorneys in both Oklahoma and Florida, but they couldn't do anything unless he returned to Florida to file suit.

George Giek, the AAA's managing director of automotive engineering, advises against getting repairs where customers are mostly transients. Try to get into a town where the shop has a local reputation to protect.

To avoid breaking down while on vacation, "the name of the game is prevention," says Giek. "Start out with an excellent operating vehicle," he warns, so that it has a chance of completing the trip. If you use gas stations without attendants, make sure you check your tires, tire pressure, and fluid levels at least every other fill-up, advises Giek. To prevent theft, he warns you to lock your car when no one is in it—even if you get out just to pump gas.

Besides watching out for crooks, also watch out for Good Samaritan mechanics who try to do repairs requiring skills or knowledge they may not possess—especially for work on electric or engine problems on newer-model cars.

The old-fashioned service station may not be able to handle

the problem, cautions Giek. What often happens, he says, is that the shop will make an effort to help people in distress, "trying to get the car mobile" and "bite off things they can't do" in the high-tech arena. He warns that service stations in national park areas are usually capable of only light repairs. He adds that cars are being towed into such stations and not being repaired correctly.

21

The New-Car Warranty Repair Rip-off

Many people buy a new car feeling secure that the warranty will take care of anything that goes wrong. Unfortunately, this is not the case. The warranties may look great on paper, but when something goes wrong, you don't always get satisfaction.

The car manufacturers are not beyond denying legitimate claims to hold down warranty costs. (Detroit's Big Three automakers spent over $9.2 billion in 1992 on warranty repairs, according to *Ward's Automotive Reports*.) Also, dealers and their mechanics may be reluctant to do warranty work because of undercompensation, mechanics may not be properly trained to repair the new cars, and it may take a long time before a thorny repair problem is figured out or parts are available.

Beyond that, industry arbitration of warranty claims is often heavily tilted against the consumer, and state lemon laws have serious limitations in most states. It could take years of court battles to get your due.

Turning over a New Leaf?

Automakers—particularly the domestic companies—have a sordid past when it comes to honoring their warranties.

In 1992, a man who had worked as a service and customer assistance representative for a U.S. automaker for 16 years until 1986 said: "I couldn't believe the arrogance toward customers and dealers. . . . Individuals who did the best job of controlling warranty by arbitrary arrogance were rewarded with promotions."

More recently, here's what the domestic companies have been up to:

General Motors had a leaking head-gasket problem on its Quad 4 engines but dragged its feet about the problem for some two years, according to *Automotive News*. The reason: Company executives couldn't agree on how to handle what would be an expensive and extensive recall. According to the *Automotive News* report, GM engineers knew the whole time how to fix the problem. Still, a recall wasn't announced until 1993, after a new regime headed by Jack Smith took over at GM.

Ford Motor Company admitted in 1993 that it takes up to a year for technicians to identify some vehicle malfunctions, forcing customers to make frequent trips to the dealer for repair of the same problem. The company also admitted that it took about six months for Ford dealers to get new parts for new-model cars.

Ford had even tried to avoid taking back a car under Michigan's lemon law, saying that it couldn't fix the car within the law's time frame because of the unavailability of parts. Ray and Phyllis Ayer had purchased a 1989 diesel pickup truck at a Ford dealer in Ann Arbor. They began to have engine troubles and met the lemon law criteria (the vehicle had been out of service for at least 30 days during the first year of ownership). The

Ayers sued and won. In 1993, the state court of appeals upheld the decision.[4]

According to *Automotive News*, as recently as mid-1993 Chrysler Corporation penalized dealers who exceeded a certain repair average on a particular warranty item for three out of five tracking periods. It wouldn't let such dealers use its electronic system for handling warranty claims, which reimbursed them within three to five days for repairs. Instead, said the newspaper, Chrysler made the dealers fill out forms by hand, a practice that could mean 60 days or more for reimbursement.

Import-car companies may be no better. Whereas Japanese and European cars "may have fewer defects," says Clarence Ditlow III, director of the Center for Auto Safety, when there's a problem the foreign automakers "are often tougher to deal with than domestic companies."

But reform is in the air. Ford said in 1993 that its customer service employees would for the first time work with engineers from the beginning on new vehicle projects. This will help ensure that cars won't pose repair difficulties and that new parts will be on hand when vehicles are introduced. Ford also said that dealers would get more technical training. In 1993, Chrysler made its first attempt to terminate the franchise of a dealer because of poor consumer satisfaction ratings.

Dealer Warranty Reimbursement

Dealers complain that they are underpaid for warranty work and that, in effect, they subsidize warranty repairs. This discourages them from wanting to do such work.

In 1992, the average dealer was losing about $40,000 annually on the difference between retail and warranty compensation, according to the National Automobile Dealers Association (NADA).

Not only do most dealers have to follow the lower warranty time allowances in the manufacturers' flat-rate manuals, but they also receive less money for parts. While the dealer retail parts markup is in the 60 to 70 percent range, the Big Three U.S. auto companies pay only a 40 percent markup for 1994 and later models, and less for older models. Dealers incur more expenses for warranty work as well.

Dealers also are not keen to do too many warranty repairs for fear that their claims will be rejected—causing them to absorb the costs or prompt a warranty audit that would disallow many past warranty payments.

One bright sign is that Ford announced in 1993 that it would allow dealers to charge it even more for labor than it charged retail customers. Also, some dealers are given discretionary money to resolve complaints—even for cars out of warranty.

Other Shady Practices

There are still more questionable practices that go on with new cars. Among them:

- *Transit damage.* A small percentage of cars get damaged while in transit from the factory to the dealer or while at the dealership. In such cases, the damaged parts may be repaired instead of replaced, or not fixed at all, and the buyer is never told. (See chapter 31 for additional information.)
- *Dealer prep.* Dealer preparation of new cars is often done by low-skilled workers and may not be done thoroughly. Only a few states, such as Arizona, Montana, Ohio, and Wisconsin, require dealers to furnish customers with a copy of the dealer prep report, showing that the work has been done.

  A few dealers engage in a practice known as "double dipping," in which they charge consumers for delivery and preparation charges. They are also reimbursed by the manufacturer.
- *Tire warranties.* Curiously, auto company warranties usually cover all parts of the car except tires, palming off that responsibility on the tire manufacturers. This often bounces consumers back and forth between the car dealer and tire dealer, trying to get someone to honor the warranty. In New Hampshire, however, auto

manufacturers are required to perform warranty obliga-
tions for new-car tires.

* *Customer service.* Customer service representatives of
the major auto companies are notorious for being un-
responsive to consumer complaints. "Dr. Gridlock," a
Washington Post columnist, in 1993, called Ford's customer assistance number and was put on hold for 37
minutes, then transferred to another number. He eventually gave up.

Excuses, Excuses, Excuses

Auto dealers and factory representatives use all kinds of
excuses for not honoring warranties. If you don't put on many
miles, they might say the problem is caused by your not driving
enough. That's the excuse that BMW of North America, Inc.,
gave to Pierre Forest of Santa Barbara, California, as to why the
battery on his $80,000 1989 BMW 750iL was almost always dis-
charged. He lived less than a mile from his office and drove the
car less than 5,000 miles in two years. However, a jury found
that BMW had willfully violated the state lemon law and awarded
Mr. Forest $172,000.[5] If, on the other hand, you drive a lot,
automakers often claim "owner abuse" is the cause of defects.

Another common excuse is to blame a "design characteris-
tic" of that model for a problem, as though that's a reason for
not fixing it. That's what Mercedes-Benz told Hilary Kaufman
of New Jersey when he complained that his car had a steering
shimmy and pulled to either side. He didn't buy their argument
and received $105,230 from the automaker under the state's
lemon law.[6]

Arbitration

The auto companies have set up arbitration procedures to
settle warranty complaints in which decisions are binding on
them but not on consumers. The effectiveness and fairness of
these procedures have been questioned by consumer advocates.

Chrysler and Ford have their own arbitration boards. Better Business Bureau Autoline arbitration is used nationally by Acura, Alfa Romeo, American General, Audi, General Motors, Honda, Hummer, Infiniti, Isuzu, Kia, Lexus, Nissan, Saturn, Toyota, and Volkswagen, and in one or more states by BMW, Jaguar, Maserati, Mazda, Mitsubishi, Peugeot, Porsche, Range Rover, Rolls-Royce, Saab, Subaru, Sterling, Suzuki, and Volvo.

The Automotive Consumer Action Program (AUTOCAP), in which some state and regional new-car dealer associations are participants, handles arbitration for BMW, Fiat, Honda, Isuzu, Jaguar, Mazda, Mitsubishi, Nissan, Rolls-Royce, Saab, and Volvo.

Decisions of the Chrysler, Ford, and BBB arbitration panels are binding on manufacturers but not on consumers. AUTO-CAP panel decisions are nonbinding, but manufacturers have voluntarily honored them.

The California Arbitration Review Board did a survey of consumers who went through arbitration in 1993 and found that only 19 percent of those who used the now-defunct American Automobile Association's Autosolve program (Toyota, Lexus, and Porsche) said they were treated fairly compared with 25 percent for Chrysler, 35 percent for General Motors (through BBB Autoline), and 47 percent for Ford. The AAA and Chrysler programs did not permit consumers to testify in person, whereas the others did. The BBB tended to mediate a high percentage of cases before going to arbitration.

"All too often," explains Clarence Ditlow of the Center for Auto Safety, "arbitration is part of a drawn-out process that wears down the consumer." (See the Appendix for arbitration contacts.)

Lemon Laws

Every state has a new-car lemon law designed to give consumers relief from cars that dealers and manufacturers can't or won't fix. Typically, lemon laws allow the manufacturer four tries or 30 days out of service to repair any defect that substantially impairs the use, value, or safety of the vehicle. After that, the automaker usually must replace the vehicle or refund the purchase price, less an allowance for use.

Most of these laws, however, are somewhat lemons themselves.

A big drawback of many of these laws is a requirement to go through manufacturer-sponsored arbitration, if available, before filing suit.

Philip R. Nowicki, who oversees lemon law arbitration for the Florida state attorney general's office, did his 1987 doctoral dissertation on lemon laws. He concluded that the process was unduly influenced by the automakers' arbitration, which he found did not comply with many critical FTC rules and had panels that by and large totally ignored the lemon laws when reaching decisions. The vast majority of awards, he found, consisted of further repair attempts rather than return of the purchase price. Since that time, he said in 1994, auto company arbitration has improved from "horrendous" to "fair to bad."

Because of such shortcomings, some 13 states have set up their own lemon law arbitration programs—although at least six of them require consumers to use automaker arbitration first.

Consumer Reports has found such state-run programs much better for consumers. It compared 1991 statistics from Better Business Bureau arbitration with data from three state-run programs to determine the percentage of consumers who went to arbitration and received a replacement vehicle or a refund. Connecticut's percentage was 77 percent; Florida's, 55 percent; and New York's, 48 percent. Nationally the BBB gave such awards to only 14 percent. The same year, Chrysler decided only 15.4 percent of arbitrations completely in favor of the consumer. As for Ford, which makes a greater effort to resolve cases before arbitration, the figure was 30 percent.

There are other shortcomings of many state lemon laws:

- Defects in most states must crop up within the first 12 months/12,000 miles, even though warranties currently last longer.
- Over 75 percent of the lemon laws allow manufacturers three, four, or more attempts to fix cars with safety defects, even though further driving of such cars could be life-endangering.

- Except for Arkansas, Kansas, and Ohio, the number of tries to fix a defective car applies to each separate problem.
- Only about 22 states have provisions for double or triple awards for certain successful consumer court suits. Such awards would encourage automakers to replace defective cars prior to a court suit.
- Only about half of the lemon laws include leased vehicles, even though leases account for about a quarter of retail new-car sales made by domestic manufacturers.

(See chapter 18 for more lemon law defects, and chapters 28 and 31 for information on suing under lemon and other laws.)

Avoiding the Warranty Rip-off

You can reduce your chances of getting a defective car and facing a warranty rip-off by following these pointers:

- *Buy cars that hold up.* Check *Consumer Reports* subscriber questionnaire survey, published each April, or consult *Consumer Reports New Car Buying Guide.* Both include reliability data for models after several years of service.

   For example, *Consumer Reports* April 1994 Reliability History index, based on subscriber data from the previous three model years, showed an alarming disparity between particular cars. For 1994 small cars, the Toyota Tercel was rated some 70 percent better than average while the Hyundai Excel was rated over 20 percent worse than average. For compact cars, the range was from 60 percent better than average for the Infiniti G20 to 60 percent worse than average for the Pontiac Sunbird.
- *Choose your dealer carefully.* Buying from the dealer who gives the best price may cost you more money in the long run. In addition to price, consider the dealer who has the best service department and will go to bat

for you in warranty disputes. Check out the dealer with your neighbors, the local Better Business Bureau, and any local or state consumer protection agency, and ask to see the dealer's consumer satisfaction index rating.

- *Try to test-drive the actual car you're going to buy before accepting delivery.* Norman Thomas of Georgia wishes he had. He test-drove one 1980 Dodge Diplomat and then bought another without test-driving it after the salesman told him it would drive as well.

  He drove no more than a block from the dealership before detecting a distinct vibration in the steering wheel—the start of years of repair problems and a lawsuit that wasn't settled in his favor until 1985.[7]

- *Make sure all defects are corrected before accepting delivery.* The dealer may tell you that a problem will go away after you drive the car awhile, or that it will be taken care of at the first maintenance check. Don't believe it.

- *Save all documentation.* Just in case you might have to go to court to get your warranty honored, save everything connected with the sale and repairs. This includes brochures, ads, requests for warranty work, and warranty repair orders.

22

Secret Warranties

According to a document received by the *Detroit News* in 1988, Toyota Motor Corporation had a reimbursement policy for 41 components that were out of warranty. The repair problems ranged from engine cylinder wear on trucks to muffler corrosion in Camrys. Unfortunately, Toyota didn't bother to notify car owners about the policy and accommodated only those who complained. Like other companies, Toyota insisted it had no secret warranty but made adjustments on a case-by-case basis.

The Center for Auto Safety estimates that at any one time the auto companies are carrying out 500 such "secret warranty" campaigns for widespread failures neither covered by the main warranty nor subject to a safety recall. Usually, only car owners who complain—often, bitterly—get free or reduced-cost repairs; those who don't complain or don't complain enough end up paying for repairs out of their own pocket.

In some instances under a secret warranty (or "goodwill adjustment," as the auto companies like to call them), the dealer might be allowed to decide on an adjustment, whereas at other times it might be the manufacturer's regional office. Sometimes even dealers don't know of such adjustments.

Several states have enacted laws against secret warranties, including California, Connecticut, Virginia, and Wisconsin. They require formal notification to all owners.

If you think your out-of-warranty car has some type of premature failure that the auto manufacturer should cover and won't, write the Center for Auto Safety (see Appendix). It may already know of a secret warranty or might use your information to discover one. The organization has smoked out many secret warranties, including peeling paint on Ford F-series trucks and General Motors cars and light trucks. Send them a letter giving the make, model, and year of your vehicle, a brief explanation of the problem, $1 to cover handling, and a self-addressed, stamped business-size envelope for a two-ounce letter. For about $25 to $30, the National Highway Traffic Safety Administration (NHTSA) will send you a printout of available service bulletins. You will then be charged an additional 10 cents a page for copies of bulletins you request. Also report any adjustments you get to the Federal Trade Commission. (See Appendix for addresses.)

If you've paid for a repair and later learn there's been a secret warranty, you can take the case to small-claims court when the manufacturer refuses to reimburse you.

23

Swindles by Design

Some repairs appear to be rip-offs by design of the auto manufacturers themselves. They make particular repairs difficult, charge high prices for parts, don't make component parts readily available, encourage parts proliferation, and don't standardize certain parts.

Most motorists don't find out about these rip-offs until they're hit with an outrageous repair bill. Nevertheless, you can get an idea what lies ahead before you buy a car by reading two annual publications, *The Complete Car Cost Guide* and *The Car Book*.

The Complete Car Cost Guide gives projected maintenance

costs for each car over the first five years. The range can be startling. For 1994 compact models, for example, lowest maintenance costs were for the Infiniti G20 ($3,012), Ford Tempo ($3,194), and Saturn SL ($3,492). The highest were for the Toyota Camry SE V6 ($6,360), Toyota Celica GT ($6,240), and Mazda 626 ES ($6,229).

"It's not the purchase price, but the amount it takes to own and operate a new vehicle that determines its true value," says Peter S. Levy, publisher of the guide.

The Car Book gives each vehicle's repair costs for parts likely to need replacing within 100,000 miles—the water pump, alternator, front brake pads, starter, fuel injection, fuel pump, struts, lower ball joints, and CV joints/universal joints.

For example, alternator replacement on 1994 compacts ranged from $191 for the Chevrolet Cavalier to $923 for the BMW 318.

The Car Book also compares maintenance costs.

Component Parts

Frequently, auto companies make you buy a whole expensive assembly when an inexpensive component breaks.

When a $5 taillight lens cracks, says Clarence Ditlow III, director of the Center for Auto Safety, many consumers are forced to replace it with a $100 modular assembly because the automaker saved "a few cents in assembly costs."

Even when a component is available, it may take a long time for a repair shop to get it; meanwhile, your car is immobilized.

Shops will sometimes put an expensive part on your car because it can be bought locally, whereas a less expensive component must be special-ordered.

Standardizing Parts

Auto companies put out so many models and make so many changes from year to year that there has been an explosion in the number of parts needed to keep the nation's cars running.

This makes parts more expensive and difficult to obtain. Ford said in 1993 that the 43 million Ford vehicles on the road use 400,000 different parts.

Jim Mancuso, a dealership service consultant in Winnetka, Illinois, says that whereas it took only five fan belts to service all the different Chevrolet models from 1949 through 1953, it now takes over 300 for the last several model years. "This proliferation of models has made it very difficult to stock the parts necessary to repair the different cars in a dealership," he says.

General Motors has been trying to get its platform groups to share an increasing number of parts. In 1992, there were 45 different catalytic converters, and GM's goal is to reduce the number to four.

Where the same parts are shared by several car lines or even car makers, they may be sold for different prices. Shop around.

24

Rip-offs
Around the Car

Let's take a tour around the car to find more potential rip-offs not already discussed.

Suspension Scams

Beware of any shop that wants to sell you coil springs, a favorite rip-off of many chains. "Coil springs generally last the life of the car," says Albert C. Bender of the district attorney's office in Santa Clara County, California.

One variation is coil-spring spacers, which are supposed to lift sagging springs. You might be told that a front-end alignment can't be done without installing them.

If a shop tries to sell you coil springs or spacers, ask for written measurements to demonstrate their need. If the shop can't come up with them, they're trying to rip you off.

Shock Absorbers

Shock absorbers are another big rip-off item. The Better Business Bureau cautions that unless you've noticed severe body sway, front-end dip when braking, and a bouncing ride, you probably don't need shock absorbers.

Electric System

Beware of shops that tell you that you need a new battery and alternator and perhaps a starter. "It's a red flag," says Fred Pirochta, director of the Repair Facility Division of the Michigan Bureau of Automotive Regulation. "I can guarantee you [that] one or two of those parts are in serviceable condition." If the shop tries to sell you more than one of the three, get a second opinion, he says.

Alternators appear to be a favorite rip-off item. In undercover runs, the district attorney's office in Nassau County, New York, was sold four unneeded alternators in 1989 and five in 1987.

Tune-ups

Never ask for a tune-up. Modern cars don't need them. They may just need replacement of spark plugs and perhaps a new distributor cap and rotor, or a diagnostic test to determine computer adjustments. Tell the mechanic the problem you're having and get a diagnostic test to determine what's wrong. You might just need a simple adjustment.

BALL JOINTS AND OTHER STEERING REPAIRS

Unnecessary replacement of ball joints is one of the favorite rip-offs of chain shops and tire dealers. It's often pitched to those who respond to low-cost front-end alignment specials. The shop will say something like, "Sorry, we can't do an alignment without replacing your ball joints."

You'll know for sure that the shop is trying to rip you off if your car is on a lift and a service person wiggles a wheel, causing it to wobble, and says that this proves you need ball joints. You might even be told that the wheel might fall off if repairs are not made. It's actually normal for the wheel to wobble under those circumstances.

To avoid being ripped off on ball joints, make sure that any shop that recommends them writes down on an estimate the measurement of wear or looseness of the ball joint. This is stated in thousandths of an inch (.001) or in millimeters. This estimate should also give the manufacturer's specifications for maximum allowance for wear or looseness.

A California regulation requires such information on invoices. When the regulation first went into effect, ball joint sales in the state reportedly dropped by 85 percent.

Be especially suspicious if your car has relatively low mileage and the shop wants to replace ball joints. They normally shouldn't have to be replaced before 70,000 to 80,000 miles.

Three other steering components are frequently replaced unnecessarily—particularly by chain stores and tire dealers. These are control pivot arms, idler arms, and tie-rod ends.

If you go in for a front-end alignment and the shop tells you the tie-rod ends or ball joints need to be replaced, "take the car and get a second or third opinion," says Fred Pirochta, director of the Repair Facility Division of the Michigan Bureau of Automotive Regulation. That's especially true, he says, if you didn't come in with any specific problem related to those repairs.

In 1994, the Automobile Protection Association (APA) in Canada took a Ford Taurus that required a four-wheel alignment to 13 shops in the Montreal area. A Goodyear outlet replaced a new tie-rod end unnecessarily, and a Canadian Tire Corporation, Ltd., outlet needlessly replaced a wheel bearing, the APA alleged. Two other Canadian Tire outlets billed for four-wheel alignments but did only two wheels, the APA said. Three other shops aligned only two wheels, although they charged less for it than the six shops that did correct, honest four-wheel alignments.

The APA says that if your tires are wearing evenly and the car tracks straight, you probably don't need a wheel alignment.

25

A Checklist for Avoiding Rip-offs

Here are still other ways to avoid being ripped off on auto repairs, plus some tips worth repeating and expanding on:

◊ *Beware of low-priced advertising, coupons, and free inspections.* Your chances of driving out with a bargain are remote.

For example, when a local auto repair shop advertised a $9 coupon to check automotive air conditioners, a man in Arizona jumped at the offer. After all, he believed in preventive maintenance. Although his car's air conditioner had worked fine for over five years, the shop owner said the compressor was shot and a new one was needed. "He told me that he just got a good deal on my type of compressor, and he would pass the savings on to me. The cost: $556." The man didn't bite, and his air conditioner was still in good working order several months later.

✓*Avoid heavily advertised repair shops.* The more they advertise, the less you should trust them. Chances are, they're going to make you pay somehow for that advertising. Your best bet is to find a shop that doesn't advertise at all but is still busy— from repeat business.

✓*Use AAA-approved shops.* American Automobile Association clubs in some 26 states and the District of Columbia have a program for members. Before approving a shop, the AAA surveys recent customers and checks its complaint record with the Better Business Bureau and government consumer affairs offices.

Shops must give a 90-day, 4,000-mile warranty on repairs, can't exceed the estimate by more than 10 percent, and must return old parts if requested. Shops must also agree to let the AAA arbitrate disputes, and the decision is binding for the shop.

In addition, technicians must be certified by the National Institute for Automotive Excellence (ASE) for the type of repairs performed, or the shop must agree to obtain such certification. Shops must have up-to-date equipment, and a supervisor must be available during service hours for member contact and quality control purposes.

✓*Use diagnostic centers or diagnostic vans that are not connected with repair shops.* That way, you'll know exactly what's wrong with your car when you take it into a repair shop.

✓*Find mechanics who ask questions.* To properly diagnose a problem, a mechanic should ask lots of questions such as: When did you first notice the problem? At what speed do you hear the noise? Does it happen when the engine is cold or warmed up? What repairs have been done in the area? Does it happen both in the rain and in dry weather?

✓*Don't ask for specific repairs.* Tell the shop what the problem is, and let the mechanic figure out what repair is needed. For example, instead of asking for a tune-up, tell the shop the car is hard to start in the morning, or is getting poor fuel mileage.

Find out if recommended repairs are for preventive maintenance or to replace a failed part. Although sometimes you can avoid future repair costs or a breakdown by replacing parts before they fail, all too often shops want to replace parts long before their time. For preventive-maintenance items, ask how much life is left in the part and what are the merits of replacing now instead of waiting.

Get more than one estimate. This is especially true for expensive repairs and for repairs with a history of rip-offs.

✓ *Have the shop put the symptoms you're complaining about on the estimate or repair order.* That way, if the symptoms still exist after the repairs, you can prove your car wasn't repaired right.

Don't give carte blanche authority to do any repair necessary. Make sure you get a written estimate. If the shop can't give a written estimate without further diagnosis, make them put a notation on the repair order to call you with an estimate. Many states either require a written estimate or make it mandatory upon your request. This is your only protection against an open-ended repair bill.

✓ *Find out what kind of parts are to be used.* Make the shop put on the estimate and the invoice whether parts are new, used, or rebuilt.

Don't let the shop do a teardown without telling you how much it will cost to reassemble. Be sure to get a written statement that the shop will restore the car to its original condition if you elect not to go ahead with repairs.

✓ *Get a copy of the repair order as soon as you sign it.* This will prevent the shop from adding repairs after you sign it.

Use mechanics who have passed industry competency tests. Make sure mechanics have passed the ASE test in the area of the car to be repaired. In addition, make sure body shop repairers and painters have taken I-CAR classes.

✓ *Become a regular customer of one shop.* Don't hop from chain to chain to get the best price or to have a muffler replaced at one chain, a brake job at another, a tune-up at yet another, and an oil change and lube somewhere else. Pick one shop and stay with it—preferably an independent shop where the owner is a certified master mechanic, belongs to a trade association, is on the premises, and has lots of certificates showing attendance at various industry-sponsored training classes.

Make preventive maintenance your mantra. This will help

avoid breakdowns and problems and thus potential rip-offs. Consult your owner's manual. In a 1993 survey of 200 master mechanics sponsored by ASE and Valvoline, the mechanics said that only 19 percent of their customers did an "excellent" or "good" job of having their cars maintained or serviced.

Also in 1993, AAA mobile diagnostic van technicians tested for free thousands of cars throughout Indiana. Failure rates were 50.3 percent for tires, 31.7 percent for lights, 28.8 percent for belts and hoses, 27.5 percent for oil, 20.1 percent for emissions, and 15.6 percent for batteries.

Keeping tires properly inflated not only helps them last longer but can prevent other problems. For a free copy of the *Consumer Tire Guide*, write: Tire Industry Safety Council, P.O. Box 3147, Medina, OH 44258. For an air pressure tire gauge, also send a check or money order for $2.50.

Insist on a warranty on repairs. Whereas laws in the Canadian provinces of Ontario and Quebec require 3-month/3,000 mile warranties on parts and labor (Quebec excludes tires, batteries, and repairs under $50), no state in the United States mandates a labor warranty. Only New York State demands a minimum written parts warranty. The warranty guarantees that the part will be fit for the ordinary purposes for which such parts are used for 3,000 miles or 90 days, whichever occurs first. It applies to all parts *except* used parts that are clearly marked as being sold "as is" and where no improvement has been attempted.

The manufacturer is required to repair any nonconformity. If it can't, it must either replace the part or refund the purchase price. The manufacturer must also pay for any shipping charges.

Consider remanufactured parts. They often sell for half of what a new part costs and might even carry a longer warranty. They're put together on an assembly line using the cores of old parts and may even be reengineered if flaws are found in the original. Typical remanufactured parts are alternators, starters, water pumps, master cylinders, and wiper motors.

Check out the reputation of the shop. Call a local or state consumer protection agency, a local consumer group, and the Better Business Bureau. *Washington Consumers' Checkbook* found in 1994 that the 55 shops with the worst complaint rates on file at local consumer offices were rated "adequate" or "superior" by only 78 percent of surveyed customers (268 shops with no complaints got those ratings from 90 percent of their customers). Residents of the San Francisco and Washington, DC, areas should consult their local *Consumers' Checkbook* for its customer surveys of auto repair shops.

It pays to shop around. Washington Consumers' Checkbook found extreme variances when it priced various repairs in 1993 and 1994. To replace the exhaust manifold on a 1987 Ford Escort GL, it received a low estimate of $240 from a Texaco station and a high estimate of $577.50 from a Ford dealer. The average was $425.08. The magazine also found that about a third of the highest-rated shops in consumer surveys were among the lowest-priced shops.

If your car is disabled, don't necessarily take the first tow truck that shows up at the scene. Some tow truck operators monitor police radio calls and go to the scene of accidents or disabled cars. They then tow the cars to unscrupulous shops, which give them a kickback.

Keep your old parts. "When in position to take possession of parts, do it," says Fred Pirochta, director of the Repair Facility Division of the Michigan Bureau of Automotive Regulation. This could help investigators determine if you were defrauded, and might help you in a court suit. State law might require you to ask for the old parts at the time your repair order is taken.

Learn the symptoms of simple repairs that you can do yourself. For example, when a vacuum hose becomes detached, an unscrupulous shop will often try to fleece you, possibly for hundreds of dollars, with a rebuilt transmission. When the Automobile Protection Association (APA) in Canada took cars with new batteries having loose connections to 11 shops in both 1992 and 1993, four shops sold or tried to sell replacement batteries each time.

Learn the lingo. Among the terms you'll find in John Edwards's *Auto Dictionary* (HP Books) are two nonexistent parts that crooked mechanics might say are causing the problem—the *Johnson rod* and the *muffler bearing.*

Take an auto repair class. At least learn enough so a mechanic can't double-talk you.

PART **II**

What to Do if You've Been Hornswoggled

26

Complaint Resolution Without a Lawsuit

If you feel you've been ripped off on repairs or on a new- or used-car purchase, several avenues are open to you short of taking your complaint to court. These include complaining to a consumer protection agency or dealer licensing authority, getting help from a consumer activist group, calling on the power of the press, and arbitration. However, before you resort to any of these possibilities, try to resolve the problem with the repair shop or the dealer.

Regarding repairs, don't start by making accusations or getting angry. This turns off most shop owners and service managers and gets you nowhere. Be calm. Take the approach that the shop made an honest mistake, and give them a chance to make amends.

Make sure you speak to someone who has the authority to help. In a dealership, discuss your problem with the service manager and, if necessary, the owner of the dealership. If you are dealing with a chain or franchise organization and you can't resolve the problem at the shop level, take your complaint to the national office.

For new-car warranty complaints, if you can't resolve the problem at the dealership level, complain to the auto manufacturer's district service representative. The phone number should be in your owner's manual. If you are still dissatisfied, contact the manufacturer's national consumer relations office.

Consumer Protection Agencies

If you suspect fraud or violation of laws and regulations, then a consumer protection agency, district attorney, state attorney general, or state insurance commission might be able to help you get restitution and put a stop to the illegal practices.

However, state and local consumer protection agencies don't have the resources to help everyone. "We're half the size we were in February 1992," said Eileen S. Brandenberg, chief investigator for the Prince George's County, Maryland, Office of Citizen and Consumer Affairs when interviewed at the end of 1993. Auto repair constitutes 30 percent of the agency's complaints—mostly about "work that wasn't done properly," she said. (See Appendix for consumer protection agencies that enforce auto repair laws and regulations.)

Complaints against new- and used-car dealers can also be lodged with state agencies or boards that license dealers.

One of the toughest dealer licensing authorities is Wisconsin's Department of Transportation. In one case, it managed to suspend a used-car dealer on grounds that it reasonably should have known the odometer had been turned back on a number of vehicles it sold. The vehicles in question were late-model, low-mileage vehicles originally purchased in Kentucky.

The department had warned Wisconsin dealers about odometer tampering on vehicles coming from Kentucky. It also said there was no reason for the Kentucky dealers to take title to the vehicles except for laundering purposes.

Many dealer licensing boards, however, are controlled by dealers and have a poor record of resolving complaints. In Colorado, a report by the Department of Regulatory Agencies found that although more than 2,500 complaints were received annually by the Division of Motor Vehicles, only about 2 percent were reviewed by the Motor Vehicle Dealer Licensing Board for final disposition. As a result, the licensing board was changed in the early 1990s; formerly consisting of four new-car dealers, three used-car dealers, and two consumers, it now has three members from each group.

On the national level, the Federal Trade Commission (FTC) won't help you with your individual complaints but might use complaints as a basis for citing a particular company for unfair or deceptive trade practices. Also, the National Highway Traffic Safety Administration (NHTSA) can help you get your car or tire recalled (see Appendix). The Environmental Protection Agency (EPA) may be of help concerning emission repairs and disputes over air-conditioning systems that use Freon (see chapters 9 and 17).

Consumer Organizations

State and local consumer organizations might be able to help you with your complaint. They include Consumer Action in San Francisco and Consumers Education and Protective Association International in Philadelphia.

Several national consumer organizations don't handle individual complaints, but they can give you helpful information or use your complaint to lobby for action on the federal and state levels.

Most prominent in the automotive field is the Center for Auto Safety. It has been instrumental in getting many cars recalled for safety defects, and has lobbied for the widespread use of air bags. The organization keeps track of suits involving lemon laws and legal decisions involving new-car warranties. It can send you a list of attorneys who handle auto-warranty and lemon-law cases. Send a self-addressed, stamped legal-size envelope (see Appendix).

Motor Voters is a political organization that was instrumental in passing California's lemon law as well as a federal law mandating air bags. More recently, it has worked on taking lemon-law arbitration out of the manufacturers' control and making it a component of state-run programs (see Appendix).

In Canada, the Automobile Protection Association (APA), with offices in Montreal and Toronto, is a membership organization that helps resolve complaints. It also initiates investigations and fights for auto repair reform and justice (see Appendix).

Some AAA clubs, including the Automobile Club of Northern California, will also try to resolve automotive-related complaints of members.

Power of the Press

Newspapers and radio and television stations have helped many motorists get justice from auto repair shops, dealers, auto manufacturers, auto insurance companies, and others.

Dozens of newspapers have help columns, often called Action Line, that are looking for interesting complaint letters. They'll call the business in question and try to get a resolution. Then they will print your complaint, the response, and what they were able to do. Some automotive columnists also try to help resolve complaints.

In addition, many radio and television stations support Call for Action, which provides volunteers to help resolve complaints of any kind. Auto repair is their top consumer complaint.

Mediation and Arbitration

Frequently, mediation and/or arbitration are the only viable alternatives to suing. However, unless the business is committed to arbitration, you will have to get it to agree to go along.

For new-car warranty problems, the auto manufacturer may provide arbitration that is binding on them but not on you (see Appendix and chapter 21). Many new-car dealers also provide arbitration for nonwarranty problems through the National Automobile Dealers Association's Automotive Consumer Action Panel (see Appendix). Although decisions are nonbinding on dealers, the dealers usually honor them.

If your complaint doesn't fall within the purview of the above, one or more private or public dispute resolution programs may be in effect in your community. For example, local Better Business Bureaus offer mediation and, if necessary, arbitration provided you can get the other side to agree. Decisions are legally binding on both parties.

More than half of the state attorneys general offer some form of alternative dispute resolution. Some of the better programs are offered in Maryland, Massachusetts, North Carolina, and Vermont.

Maryland's state attorney general's office has had a binding arbitration service since 1978 and has resolved more than 3,000 cases.

Several district attorneys also have mediation and arbitration services. In Florida, the state attorney's office in Jacksonville has a program in which retired business people, attorneys, or judges mediate consumer disputes.

Many small-claims courts also provide arbitration.

27

Overcoming Mechanic Liens and Withholding Payment

Whereas few state laws protect you against incompetent and crooked mechanics, most state mechanic lien laws protect incompetent and crooked mechanics from you. These laws allow mechanics, including the botch artists and con artists, to hold your car (and in some cases, allow them to sell it) unless you pay up. It's like holding your car for ransom.

Only a few states disallow a mechanic's lien under certain circumstances. In Washington State, for example, a shop can't impose a mechanic's lien on unauthorized parts or labor if it fails to comply with the laws involving estimates, return of parts, and required signs. In one case, a car owner was convicted of second-degree theft for taking his own car from a repair shop without paying the $850 bill. However, the decision was overturned by the state court of appeals because the shop didn't give a written estimate. The state supreme court upheld that opinion but said the car owner still owed the money since, under state law, absence of a written estimate prohibits only a mechanic's lien, not payment.[8]

Rhode Island and Louisiana limit liens to written and authorized estimates. Alaska, Connecticut, Florida, Idaho, and Wisconsin prohibit mechanics from taking possession of vehicles in lieu of payment for unauthorized repairs. In Florida, Michigan, and Nevada, shops must comply with state auto repair laws to have rights to a lien. California, Hawaii, and Michigan require the shop to be licensed in order to impose a lien.

If your state has no law to protect you against a lien and you feel you've been ripped off, pay by credit card. You could get relief later under the federal Fair Credit Billing Act, which allows you to withhold payment for the part of the bill in dispute if two conditions are met: (1) the amount of the transaction exceeds $50, and (2) the transaction has taken place in the state where you reside, or within 100 miles of the address you use on your credit card.

No such restrictions apply if your transaction was with the issuer of the credit card, with someone directly or indirectly controlled by the issuer, or with a franchisee of the issuer's products or services. This would mean that no restrictions would apply if you used a Texaco credit card at a Texaco station, a General Motors card at a GM dealer, or a Sears card at a Sears auto repair center. There are also no restrictions if the credit card issuer solicited you by mail or participated in a solicitation to use your credit card to purchase the particular product or service.

Before contacting the credit card issuer to withhold payment, you must make a good-faith attempt to resolve the problem with the merchant who accepted your credit card. Send letters by certified mail to both the credit card company and the repair shop telling them why you are withholding the money. Even if your transaction doesn't meet the requirements of the law, contact your credit card company to try to resolve the dispute. They may be willing to work something out.

In Texas, a lien on a motor vehicle continues if you stop payment on a check, and the shop can eventually regain possession of your car. The Maine state attorney general's office advises car owners to never pay a disputed bill in that state by check and then stop payment because you could be charged with "theft of services"—a criminal offense. It may be wiser, says the attorney general's office, to pay the bill and file a claim in small-claims court.

Even in states that allow you to stop payment on a check and to keep your car, there will still be a lien on your car until the dispute is settled.

Posting a Bond

If the repair shop has your car and you refuse to pay the bill, many states allow you to go to court and post a bond—sometimes for twice or more of the amount owed—and get your car back. For example, in Virginia you can pay a bond equal to the lien and court costs, and in Maryland you can file a corporate bond for double the amount of the disputed bill in the county where the services or materials were provided, then claim your automobile. The other party then has six months to file suit or the bond is discharged.

Florida has one of the best of these laws. There, consumers can get their car back by filing a cash or surety bond for the amount of the repair bill owed, plus accrued storage charges. The shop then has 60 days to file suit to recover the bond, or the money is returned to the motorist. Consumers winning such a suit may be entitled to damages plus court costs and attorney's fees. Those who stop payment on a check or credit card have no recourse to this law.

Oklahoma mandates attorney's fees to winners of lien enforcement suits, whereas New Mexico provides them at the court's discretion.

28

Suing the #?&$%@*: An Overview of Three All-Purpose Laws

If you've been ripped off over an auto repair, a used car, or a new car, you've got quite a few laws to fall back on.

Three basic laws that cover all three types of purchases are described in this chapter. Specific information and examples of important legal decisions using these and other laws are included in the following chapters.

Some of these laws can be used in small-claims court without a lawyer, whereas some may provide attorney's fees and court costs if you win.

Deceptive Trade Practices

All states have laws against unfair and deceptive trade practices. These laws allow the attorney general and sometimes other law enforcement officials to file suit against businesses that violate the laws. All states except Arkansas and Iowa allow consumers to use these laws to file suit on their own. According to Eugene D. De Santis, former counsel to the New York Assembly's Consumer Protection Committee, the idea behind these so-called private rights of action is to "turn loose an army of little attorneys general who would go out and clean up the marketplace."

Whereas many states allow you to collect only actual damages, some states want to discourage unfair practices and allow for a minimum award or even double or triple damages under certain circumstances. For example, Utah mandates a minimum $2,000 award; Idaho, $1,000. North Carolina and the District of Columbia allow automatic treble damages, and Wisconsin automatic double damages. In addition, some states, such as Texas, have mandatory coverage of attorney's fees and costs if you win such a suit. (Texas also allows actual damages plus double or triple actual damages that do not exceed $1,000.)

Although some states generically prohibit unfair and deceptive practices, most states spell out what is specifically prohibited. The following are among the most widespread provisions of these laws:

- A company represents that goods are original or new when they are deteriorated, altered, reconditioned, reclaimed, used, or secondhand.
- A company represents that goods or services are a particular standard, quality or grade, or that goods are a particular style or model, when they are of another.
- A company represents that goods or services have sponsorship, approval, characteristics, ingredients, uses, benefits, or qualities that they do not have.

- A company advertises goods or services with intent not to sell them as advertised.
- A company makes a false or misleading statement of fact concerning the reasons for, existence of, or amount of price reductions.

Some states go further, with specific laws concerning repairs or services in general.

Knowingly making a false or misleading statement of fact concerning the need for replacement or repair, or else representing that repairs are needed when they are not, is prohibited in Alabama, Alaska, California, the District of Columbia, Idaho, Indiana, Kansas, Maryland, Michigan, Nevada, New Mexico, Ohio, Pennsylvania, Tennessee, Texas, Virginia, and Wyoming.

Misrepresenting the ability to deliver or complete a consumer transaction within a stated period of time is covered in the laws of Indiana, Michigan, and Oregon.

Gross overcharges are prohibited in Michigan and New Mexico.

Uniform Commercial Code

Every state except Louisiana (see below) uses provisions of the Uniform Commercial Code (UCC) in dealing with express and implied warranties of goods and services and the rejection and revocation of acceptance of goods.

An *express warranty* is any fact or promise made by the seller or any description of the goods or sample or model that is made part of the basis of the bargain. This would include the written warranty, brochures, advertisements that promise something, etc.

However, not all seller's statements are express warranties. Some are considered "puffing," and thus not actionable. For example, the New Jersey Supreme Court ruled in 1991 that the advertising slogan "You're in good hands with Allstate" was puffing and couldn't be used to prove fraud.[9] Courts may make exceptions to puffing statements if the buyer is not expected to be as knowledgeable about a product as the seller.

Implied warranties come in two major varieties:

1. Implied warranty of merchantability means that goods must be fit for the ordinary purposes for which such goods are used. A person suing must show that the goods were defective when they left the possession of the manufacturer or seller. The merchantability aspect can cover such things as defects that crop up after the written warranty, so long as it's reasonable to assume that such defects shouldn't occur.
2. Implied warranty of fitness for a particular purpose occurs when the buyer relies on the seller's skill or judgment that a product is fit for a particular purpose. The test is that the seller must have known at the time of sale the particular use for which the goods were intended and must have known that the buyer was relying on the seller.

Sellers often exclude or modify the implied warranty in their contracts. However, to do this, the disclaimer must be conspicuous and the seller cannot engage in any unconscionable act at the time of sale.

Sellers of new goods are not allowed to modify or disclaim the implied warranty of merchantability or fitness for a particular purpose in Connecticut, the District of Columbia, Kansas, Maine, Maryland, Massachusetts, Mississippi, Vermont, and West Virginia.

The same implied warranty protection is provided to used-car buyers in the above states—with two exceptions: Connecticut excludes vehicles selling for under $3,000. In Mississippi, protection extends only to used vehicles six model years old or less that have been driven 75,000 miles or less. (However, Mississippi does offer protection in cases where proper disclosure of the disclaimer has not been given.) In addition, California offers implied warranty protection—when an express warranty is given—for a minimum 30 days or the length of the express warranty (up to three months).

When goods don't conform to the express or implied warranty, you can either reject them before acceptance or revoke acceptance within a reasonable time after discovering the nonconformity or after you should have discovered it.

The UCC treats those who reject goods before accepting them differently from those who revoke acceptance afterward.

According to the New Jersey Supreme Court, before acceptance the buyer can reject goods for any nonconformity; after acceptance, the nonconformity must "substantially" impair the value of the goods. Also, before acceptance the burden is on the seller to prove that the nonconformity has been corrected, whereas after acceptance the burden is on the buyer to prove a defect.[10]

In Louisiana, there is *redhibition*, which is defined as the "avoidance of a sale on account of some vice or defect in the thing sold, which renders it either absolutely useless, or its use so inconvenient and imperfect, that it must be supposed that the buyer would not have purchased it, had he known of the vice."

Magnuson-Moss

The Magnuson-Moss Warranty–Federal Trade Commission Improvement Act is a federal law covering warranties on consumer products, including cars and car parts. It allows you to file suit for damages and get other legal and equitable relief in either state or federal court if a supplier, warrantor, or service contractor fails to comply with the law or any written or implied warranty or service contract.

To file in federal court, the amount in controversy must be $25 or more for individual claims and $50,000 or higher in a class action. (A class action suit must have at least 100 plaintiffs.)

If you win such a suit, the law says the court "may" allow you to collect reasonable attorney's fees based on actual time expended. However, in 1989 the West Virginia Supreme Court said that courts around the country have taken the view that those who prevail in a breach-of-warranty suit for revocation of acceptance under state UCC laws can recover reasonable attorney's fees under the Magnuson-Moss Act.[11]

The act requires warranties to be labeled "full" or "limited." With a full warranty, the manufacturer must fix a defective product, without charge, within a reasonable time and a reasonable number of tries or give you a choice of a replacement or your money back. Also, the implied warranty of merchantability or fitness for a particular purpose can't be disclaimed or modified. You can also use the product while the case is in litigation.

With a limited warranty, which auto manufacturers presently provide, you are entitled to implied warranty protection during the length of the written warranty. However, such protection can be extended if the warrantor's limitation was unconscionable and not set forth in clear and unmistakable language and prominently displayed on the face of the warranty.

If you buy a service contract from the supplier of a product within 90 days of purchase, the law also prohibits the supplier from disclaiming or modifying the implied warranty.

29

Suing Auto Repair Shops

Unfair or deceptive trade practices and express and implied warranties under the uniform commercial code (see chapter 28) are often used to settle auto repair service complaints, as are state or local auto repair laws and state contract laws.

Many disputes can be settled in small-claims court.

In one Louisville, Kentucky, small-claims court case in 1989, a man had bought a service contract for $350 along with his new car. Nearly two years later, while on a trip, he paid $584 to have the air conditioner fixed. The warrantor refused to reimburse him, claiming he was obligated under the terms of the warranty to get prior approval for repairs. The man said he wasn't aware of that provision because he had not been given a copy of the warranty. The warrantor's attorney argued that the application he signed included a statement that the buyer had read a copy of the agreement. Nevertheless, the car owner produced stacks of invoices and letters to support his case, and the judge accepted his argument that he was never shown or given an actual policy. However, the judge didn't award him the cost of the repairs. Instead, he awarded him $350—the cost of the policy.

Deceptive Practices

Many auto repair cases come under state unfair and deceptive practice acts. For example, if a repair doesn't fix the problem and the shop won't give you your money back, you can sue under such an act. In Louisiana, Ulysses Joseph did just that. In 1986, he took his 1982 car to the Transmission Center in Baton Rouge because of a serious vibration problem. The manager said that the transmission was causing the problem and charged $1,469.70 for repairs. After Joseph drove one block and found the car still vibrated, he was told he would have to pay for additional repairs. He was convinced he had been cheated, found out he didn't have a transmission problem, and eventually had the vibration fixed elsewhere for $327.04 (it turned out to be a problem with the flywheel). The court awarded him the $1,469.70 he paid for repairs, $500 for inconvenience, and $1,000 in attorney's fees and interest.[12]

Sally G. Young of South Carolina successfully used her state's unfair trade practices law in a body shop/insurance company dispute. Her 1985 Honda was involved in a wreck in 1986. American Mutual Insurance Company, the other driver's insurer, gave her the option of either declaring the car a total and paying her $11,500 or having it repaired. She received an estimate from Century Lincoln-Mercury indicating that the car could be fixed as good as new for $6,900, so she authorized repairs. After completing half the work, Century found it would be necessary to make additional repairs for $2,340.11. The dealer got the go-ahead from the insurance company but not from Young. She refused to endorse over the check from the insurance company to the dealer. She claimed she would not have authorized repairs had she known they were going to cost more than the $6,900, and that her car was worth less than that as a total (a used-car dealer said it was worth $9,500 retail and about $2,000 less wholesale).

Young ended up getting the insurance money, was made to pay for the estimated repairs, and was awarded $3,500 in damages, which was trebled under the law to $10,500. She also received $4,500 in punitive damages and attorney's fees of $7,352.50.[13]

In a landmark decision that involved botched repairs to a mobile home but could apply to bad auto repairs, the Texas Supreme Court in 1987 affirmed a lower court ruling that repairs carry an implied warranty under that state's Deceptive Trade Practices Act, which specifies that repair work will be done in a good and workmanlike manner. It defined good and workmanlike as "that quality of work performed by one who has the knowledge, training, or experience necessary for the successful practice of a trade or occupation and performed in a manner generally considered proficient by those capable of judging such work."[14]

Uniform Commercial Code

An Indiana court found that an AAMCO Transmissions shop's advertisement of "one day service in most cases" was an express warranty. It also found that consumers do not have to give a repair shop a chance to redo botched repairs if they have no faith in the shop's repair ability and that shop gives an unconditional warranty that says nothing about having to give it another chance.

Air System, Inc., owner of a service van, said it had relied on AAMCO's advertisement and was told repairs would take one or two days. AAMCO couldn't obtain a second gear, and Air System, a mechanical service contractor that needed the van for its business, got it themselves. AAMCO didn't return the vehicle for two weeks. When Air System finally picked up the van, the driver immediately had problems with terrible vibrations and first gear—problems that weren't present when the van was brought in. Air System wouldn't give AAMCO another chance to fix the vehicle, and the warranty didn't require it. Air System won $2,131.[15]

Under the Uniform Commercial Code, you can also revoke acceptance for a defective major part used in repairs. In 1992, the Idaho Court of Appeals ruled that consumers are not only entitled to what they paid for the defective part but can also revoke acceptance for the whole contract and collect what they paid to have their old part removed and the new part installed. Annet and Marvin Berning had Bill Drumwright install a secondhand engine he had obtained for their Chevrolet van for $1,100. It turned out that the engine was not the correct engine for the van, and it consumed oil. The Bernings had someone else install a newly rebuilt engine and sued Drumwright in small-claims court. They were awarded the $1,100 they paid for the engine and labor—less $250 for the core value of the engine, plus costs and a statutory attorney's fee of $25. Drumwright appealed twice and was ordered to pay costs and attorney's fees for the appeals.[16]

Auto Repair Laws

If you live in one of the states that have laws or regulations concerning auto repair (see chapter 7), you may be able to sue over violations. Colorado law provides triple damages or a minimum $150 award; Wisconsin mandates double damages plus costs and attorney's fees; and Michigan requires the same for willful and flagrant violations. In Utah, winning a claim against the bond of a body shop entitles one to attorney's fees.

Several states, including California, New Jersey, and Pennsylvania, require written estimates, or have the consumer sign a menu of estimate options prior to repairs. Courts in these states have continually held that if the shop fails to give a written estimate or the required options, the customer need not pay—even when the customer is obviously trying to skip out on the bill.[17]

Some states, such as Maryland and Michigan, require certain parts to be returned (see chapter 7). In a 1981 decision, the Maryland Court of Appeals ruled that a customer doesn't have to pay for the parts or labor for replacing parts not returned. The case involved a Cadillac owned by Design & Funding, Inc., which was taken to Betz Garage, Inc., because of a grinding noise. The shop did $672.16 worth of repairs. Design & Funding thought the bill preposterous and asked for the old parts but got only one part representing 3.9 percent of the repairs. Although the trial court found the repairs were necessary and authorized and ruled in favor of the garage, the appeals court said Design & Funding didn't have to pay for 96.1 percent of the bill.[18]

30

Suing Used-Car Dealers

If you buy a used car "as is" or with an expired warranty, the courts will generally hold you responsible for fixing any defects. However, if a defect causes death or injury, several state courts, such as the Montana Supreme Court and the Minnesota Court of Appeals, have generally held that dealers are responsible for the accident when such defects should have been discovered by the dealer in an inspection of the vehicle.[19]

Nevertheless, there are circumstances under which you can hold the dealer responsible if nonaccident repair problems crop up on a used car sold "as is" or with an expired warranty.

Implied Warranties

If you live in one of the states where sellers cannot exclude, modify, or limit the implied warranty of merchantability on a used car (see chapter 28), or you bought a service contract from the dealer, you may be in luck.

In Kansas, LaVerne L. Dale bought a 1978 Buick LeSabre Custom in 1981 from King Lincoln-Mercury in Wichita. The car had 32,795 miles on it. She paid almost $5,000 for the car, which was described as a "cream puff." It came with a "30-day or 1,000-mile warranty, 100 percent on driveline and air conditioner." Twenty-two days later the transmission failed and the dealer paid $468 for repairs under warranty. About 30 days later—with the warranty expired—the motor failed on a trip, and Dale had the engine block replaced for $1,218.28. She wanted the dealer to pay. It was learned that the engine had been repaired five times in 1979 before the dealer acquired it. Dale was saved by her state's implied warranty protection. The Kansas Supreme Court in 1984 said that "a relatively low mileage General Motors full-size automobile, represented by the dealer as being in excellent condition when sold, certainly can be expected to contain a motor and transmission which will give the new purchaser more than a few days' service. Such a vehicle with defective major components is patently unmerchantable."[20]

If you buy a service contract from a used-car dealer within 90 days of purchase, the Magnuson-Moss Act gives you implied-warranty protection. This means that even if the dealer's warranty or service contract doesn't cover problems, the implied warranty might.

This federal law rescued Khalid Ismael. In 1989, he purchased "as is" a used 1985 Ford Tempo from Goodman Toyota in Raleigh, North Carolina, and paid $695 for a service contract.

Unfortunately, the car spent more time in Goodman's service department than on the road. During the first four months of ownership, Ismael had to return the car for repairs at least six times and had the use of it for less than two weeks. He was not charged for repairs and each time was assured the car was fixed. However, he was never able to keep the car for more than three days before having to return it for repairs.

Ismael then spent over $900 trying to get the car repaired correctly elsewhere, but to no avail. He was told that sludge in the engine made the car unrepairable. He then sued, claiming the dealer had breached the implied warranty of merchantability because the car was unroadworthy and unrepairable at the time of purchase.

A trial judge ruled against Ismael on the grounds that he bought the car "as is," but the North Carolina Court of Appeals overturned that decision in 1992. It said the implied warranty provision for service contracts in the Magnuson-Moss Act overrode the fact that the car was sold "as is."[21]

Express Warranty Suits

You may be able to win a suit under your state's Uniform Commercial Code for breach of the express warranty of a car sold "as is." In Nebraska, George W. Warner III and Virginia C. Warner did so. In 1986, they purchased from Reagan Buick, Inc., what was described as a "one-owner" 1983 Buick Riviera. They paid $12,647 plus another $4,474 in additional costs. Shortly after taking possession, the windows either stopped working properly or made the interior lights go on when they did work. Also, the transmission didn't work correctly and the car leaked when left out in the rain. The dealer wouldn't take the car back.

It was learned that the car had been stolen, stripped, burned, and then rebuilt, passing through several hands. Expert appraisers testified that the car contained Riviera parts from various model years from 1978 to 1983, and possibly parts from other makes of cars. They also said that bundles of wires weren't attached to anything and that a 1979 instrument panel was installed without a required turbo indicator.

At the trial, the couple was awarded $7,734 from Reagan— with a dealer that previously owned the car paying half—and $1,000 each in attorney's fees from both dealers. The dealers appealed, but the decision was upheld by the Nebraska Supreme Court in 1992. The court said that evidence showed the car was only a skeleton of a 1983 Buick Riviera and was a mishmash of assorted parts, which was "sufficient evidence of a breach of an express warranty."[22]

Deceptive Trade Practices

At least two state supreme courts have ruled that similar cases fall under state deceptive practices laws. The Tennessee Supreme Court in 1992 ruled in favor of Darrell W. Morris, who in 1985 bought "as is" what was described as a 1979 Ford pickup truck that, undisclosed to him, had been wrecked or dismantled and later reconstructed. Morris didn't find out until three years later, when he received the title after paying off a loan on the car. He figured the reconstruction reduced the market value by 30 to 50 percent. The dealer, Mack's Used Cars & Parts, Inc., claimed the car was sold "as is," so it wasn't responsible. A trial court agreed and dismissed the case—a decision affirmed by an appeals court. However, the state high court overturned the ruling.[23]

Likewise, the Vermont Supreme Court, in a 1989 decision, ruled that it was a "material misrepresentation" to call a used Saab a 1974 model, when much of it was a 1972 model that had been clipped on to it.[24]

In a different type of case, Frank R. Roberts III sued under Delaware's Uniform Deceptive Trade Practices Act when a dealer's sales manager misrepresented that the service contract on a used car gave protection against major repairs. He was awarded $2,728.12, which was tripled under the law to $8,184.36. He also got $5,700 in attorney's fees, plus interest and costs.[25]

Federal Odometer Law

You could get back some of the money you paid for an "as is" used-car purchase if the dealer failed to adhere to the odometer requirements of the federal Motor Vehicle Information and Cost Savings Act or federal disclosure regulations (see chapter 19).

In Virginia, a dealer certified an odometer reading when it

had knowledge that the mileage had probably been altered, even though it didn't do the rollback itself. As a result, Mary Ann Boyd Oettinger, on a $7,000 car, was awarded $1,756.40 actual damages—tripled under the law to $5,269.20. She also received mandatory attorney's fees and court costs.[26]

Also saved was 19-year-old Barry M. Williams. A Louisiana dealer had sold him two cars without odometer statements. He first bought a 1980 Toyota Tercel with 34,367 miles on it for $4,100, but he totaled it in a one-car accident. He then bought "as is" a 1975 BMW 2002 with 54,124 miles on the odometer for $3,565.51. It turned out to be a lemon.

Williams was awarded $4,500 for the Tercel—triple the amount he overpaid, as required by law—because of the dealer's intent to defraud. When the dealer bought the Tercel from another dealer, it received a statement that the mileage on the odometer could not be relied upon. When the previous dealership bought the car, it received an odometer disclosure statement saying that there was 66,124 miles on it. Thus, either the dealer, an auction that handled the transfer, or the selling dealer rolled back the mileage.

For the BMW, which developed a plethora of problems soon after purchase, Williams was awarded the minimum $1,500 allowed under the law for the dealer's failure to disclose that the actual mileage was unknown. He also got back his purchase price and incidental expenses because the dealer didn't properly disclaim a state law, and he picked up attorney's fees under both federal and state laws.[27]

31

New-Car Suits

If your new car is defective, there are many laws under which to sue: lemon laws, uniform commercial codes, deceptive trade practices, the Magnuson-Moss Warranty Act, and transit damage.

Lemon Laws

Your state's lemon law might actually give you rights that your warranty doesn't grant you. In 1993, a New Jersey appeals court ruled that a consumer doesn't have to prove a violation of a warranty in order to prove that a car is a lemon.

The case involved a leased 1991 Toyota Corolla that stalled when it had less than a half-tank of gas and was parked in the lessee's driveway, facing downhill at about a 30-degree angle.

The court ruled that the problem substantially impaired the use of the vehicle and that the car had been presented at least three times for repair—all that was needed to get a refund or replacement under the state's lemon law.[28]

In a Louisiana case, a defective paint job was ruled a non-conformity under that state's lemon law. Norvel Williams filed suit against Chrysler Corporation and Parish-Bankston Chrysler-Plymouth-Dodge, Inc., where he bought a 1984 Chrysler LeBaron for $11,618.50. Bubbles appeared on painted surfaces covering 60 to 75 percent of the vehicle. Chrysler had the car repainted twice, but Williams was dissatisfied. He took the case to Chrysler's Customer Satisfaction Board, which ruled that the minor deficiencies should be corrected. Williams rejected the decision and sued. He was awarded the purchase price, collateral costs, and finance charges, less an allowance for use— plus $2,500 in attorneys' fees. Chrysler appealed, contending a defective paint job cannot be considered a nonconformity under the lemon law. The company estimated the vehicle could be touched up for $200 to $250. However, a court of appeals ruled that Chrysler already had the car out of service for 40 days for repainting alone—10 days more than what was called for under the lemon law. The state supreme court denied an appeal.[29]

Uniform Commercial Code

The Uniform Commercial Code (UCC) can be used if your circumstances don't meet the criteria of lemon laws or you don't want to go through the lemon-law process. For example, the UCC can be used after the lemon-law period. It can also be helpful if you don't want to wait for so many tries, so many days out of service, or to go through arbitration.

Although under lemon laws your case is against the manufacturer, the Michigan Court of Appeals said in 1991 that a majority of courts "have held that (under the UCC) the remedy of revocation of acceptance is not available against a manufacturer," but only against the seller.[30]

Under the UCC, you may be able to reject ownership before accepting a new vehicle. Ernest and Adele Ramirez did so. In 1978 they bought a camper from Autosport of Somerville, New Jersey, for $14,100—less a $4,700 trade-in allowance. They twice came to pick up the van, which they wanted for a summer vacation, and found that the van was not ready. They were called some weeks later and told the camper was ready. When they came, they were told to wait, and did so for one and a half hours, finally leaving in disgust. They eventually sued and were able to rescind the contract and recover the $4,700 for their trade-in. The ruling was affirmed by the New Jersey Supreme Court, which said that before acceptance, the buyer can reject goods for any nonconformity.[31]

Once you accept the car and it proves to be a lemon, you must revoke acceptance within a reasonable time after discovering the defect or illegal practice, or within a reasonable time during which you should have discovered it—and before any substantial change in the condition of the vehicle. Courts have widely interpreted what constitutes a reasonable time. In a case in Sandusky County, Ohio, Sue Andrews was able to revoke acceptance after driving her new 1986 Pontiac Sunbird for 9,000 miles. The salesman at Scott Pontiac Cadillac GMC, Inc., had told Andrews that the car had been involved in an accident and had sustained in excess of $500 in damage. She had problems with the car and asked just how much damage had been done. She got a copy of the repair estimate, which put the cost between $3,900 and $4,000. She filed suit as soon as she discovered the facts.[32]

In a landmark case, the Alabama Supreme Court in 1991 affirmed a lower court ruling that the UCC's allowance of damages for "injury to the person" can be interpreted to allow damages for mental anguish caused by breach of warranty. The case involved Edwin O. Dillard who purchased a new 1987 Volkswagen Scirocco for $16,449.56 in Montgomery. The car needed constant warranty work and tended to cut off and stop when he pulled out in front of oncoming traffic. Sometimes the car just stopped, and he would have to pull it off the road and wait for it to cool off for as long as 15 to 20 minutes. Once it "died," and he had to walk home (which took three hours). A jury awarded him $7,000 actual damages plus $8,000 for mental anguish. The supreme court, in agreeing with that verdict, pointed out that Dillard had suffered "anxiety, embarrassment, anger, fear, frustration, disappointment, and worry (not to mention the undisputed facts that the automobile has not been reliable or dependable and has not provided him with safe transportation)."[33]

You can also sue under the UCC for violation of the implied warranty of merchantability or the implied warranty of fitness for a particular use (see chapter 28). The particular use aspect is illustrated by the case of Felicitas Garnica of Texas, who wanted a vehicle to tow an Airstream trailer she had ordered. The dealership sales manager called Airstream to get specifications of the trailer and told Garnica that a 1987 Jeep Cherokee could do the job. However, it soon became evident that the engine of the Jeep was not large enough to pull the 23-foot trailer. The vehicle was in for repairs, including transmission work, quite often. Soon the driveshaft of the vehicle broke. Both the dealer and Jeep Eagle Sales Corporation refused to fix it, saying the breakdown was due to misuse. However, the trial court ruled that the dealer had violated the implied warranty for a particular use as well as engaging in deceptive practices. The court of appeals awarded Garnica $336,217.75, including $210,000 in punitive damages, plus interest and attorney's fees.[34]

Deceptive Trade Practices

You may be able to sue under your state's deceptive trade practices act for new-car problems. That's the way David Vincent Dickenson went. He bought a new 1982 Mercedes from Ryan Oldsmobile, Inc., in Fort Worth, Texas, and within three weeks a substantial number of defects surfaced. One was a faulty transmission, which was replaced at least twice and still had problems. Other defects included squeaky brakes, rattles in the dashboard, and low fuel mileage. Ryan had represented that the Mercedes was of the highest quality and the best the company had yet produced, and that it would get 33 mpg on the highway and 27 mpg in town. The jury found that Ryan had represented that the car or repair services were of a particular standard, quality, or grade when they were of another—a violation of the Deceptive Trade Practices Act. Also, Mercedes's failure to provide proper replacement parts was deemed "unconscionable" under the act in that it resulted "in a gross disparity between the value received and consideration paid." Mercedes had to pay $8,679.30 in actual damages, $9,000 in additional damages, and attorney's fees.[35]

If a dealer fails to tell you about transit damage to your new car, it could fall under your state's deceptive practices law.

When Rocco Pirozzi bought a new 1986 Cadillac Eldorado coupe from a dealer in Pennsylvania, the salesman didn't tell him the car had sustained a 3½-inch gouge on one of the doors in transit from the factory. The door had subsequently been repaired and repainted. Pirozzi didn't learn of the repair until two days after accepting delivery of the car from Cowan Olds-Cadillac-GMC, when another Cadillac dealer noticed the paint job.

After consulting a body shop, Pirozzi returned the car to the dealer and demanded a full refund. The dealer then had the door repainted without consulting him and delivered the car back to him. Pirozzi refused to take it back. After nearly a year at the dealership, General Motors Acceptance Corporation, which had given him a loan for the car, repossessed it and auctioned it off for less than it was owed. It then got a deficiency judgment against Pirozzi for over $4,000.

Pirozzi sued and lost, even though the dealership admitted it had a policy of not revealing damage to vehicles sustained in transit unless it was asked. That decision, however, was overturned by the Pennsylvania Superior Court in 1992. It ruled that the state's Unfair Trade Practices and Consumer Protection Law prohibits representing anything as new that is "deteriorated, altered, reconditioned, reclaimed, used or secondhand." The court also pointed out that the law considers as an unfair or deceptive act any "conduct which creates a likelihood of confusion or misunderstanding."[36]

Note: At least 14 states have specific laws or regulations concerning damage to new cars prior to delivery. These states require dealers to notify you if transit damage has exceeded a certain percentage of the manufacturer's suggested retail price—usually 3 to 6 percent—or a certain dollar amount, often $300 to $500. Typically, such easily replaced items like glass, tires, and bumpers are excluded if they are replaced with identical original equipment. Idaho and Virginia require the disclosure of all uncorrected damage, regardless of cost.

Holder in Due Course

If you financed your car through the dealer, the Federal Trade Commission's "holder in due course" rule allows you, while the warranty is in effect, to stop making payments on your car loan while you sue to get a new car or a refund.

PART  III

Consumer Reports
Survey

32

Repairing Mufflers, Brakes, and Transmissions

On the 1993 Annual Questionnaire to subscribers, *Consumer Reports* asked about muffler, brake, and transmission repairs that had been done since 1991. Some 12,000 people replied concerning muffler repairs, 22,000 about brakes, and 6,000 about transmissions. The respondents told:

- Why they chose one type of repair shop over another
- How much they were influenced by advertising—and whether they thought the ads were misleading
- Whether they received an estimate before the repair work

was done, and how accurate the estimate proved to be
- What they actually paid
- Whether they were subjected to a sales pitch for extra work
- Whether the repairs were satisfactory, and whether the repair shop satisfactorily resolved any remaining problems

The Ratings do not include individual local garages or dealerships, but as a class they are compared with the leading repair chains like Midas and Goodyear, and with car dealers' service departments.

Think Independent

Whether the problem was with the brakes, muffler, or transmission, one thing was clear: The readers who went to independent repair shops were, on average, most satisfied with the results. The Ratings give the details. In general, the survey found that well over two-thirds of those people who went to independent garages for brake or muffler repairs were repeat customers, compared with about half of those who went to chains and dealerships for repairs.

"YOU'RE NOT GONNA PAY A LOT": WHAT THE ADS SAY AND DON'T SAY

For years, Midas Muffler and Brake Shops ran ads that growled, "Nobody beats Midas. Nobody." Rival Meineke repeated the mantra with the slogan, "You're not gonna pay a lot for this muffler." Lately, Midas has taken a softer tack with glowing testimonials from customers who write sweet "Dear Midas" letters, while Meineke spokesperson George Foreman gamely tries to pretend that muffler repair and boxing have something in common. But although the words may change, the promise of low prices remains the repair chains' primary drawing card.

In the survey nearly one-third of the readers who went

to chains for muffler repairs, and almost one-fourth of those who used a chain for brake repair, said they were drawn by ads that promised low prices. (Advertising was rarely a factor for people who went to independent garages or dealerships for repairs.) But what the ads said and what the chains did were not always the same.

Midas promises to meet or beat any competitor's price, but there's a catch: You must first get a competitor's written estimate, then take it to Midas. So if you don't shop around, the Midas estimate may not be the lowest. In the experience of *Consumer Reports* readers, Midas usually charged a few dollars more than other chains.

Another theme in the ads is prompt, attentive service. According to the readers, however, prompt service is the norm. Both independent garages and chains fixed mufflers when promised 95 percent of the time. And for brake jobs, independent garages had the car ready when promised 93 percent of the time, a slightly better record than that of new-car dealers or chains.

Survey Results

As published in *Consumer Reports*, September 1994.

Brakes

According to the respondents, independent garages didn't do perfect brake work. They took a little longer to fix the car than franchised repair chains, and they more often neglected to give a written estimate. But the independent local mechanics did more satisfactory repairs—and they charged less than either dealerships or chains. The median price for a brake repair was $150 at a garage, $180 at a chain, and $200 at a dealer.

Judging from the readers' responses, local garages draw much more repeat business than do chains or dealerships. Three-fourths of the people who used a local garage had been there before, compared with 61 percent for chains and 56 percent for dealerships.

Nearly 30 percent of the readers who used a chain did so

because they had been attracted by an ad. Of them, 28 percent thought the ad was misleading, most often because the advertised price didn't cover the cost of extra parts.

The better chains, in terms of overall satisfaction, were Car-X, Meineke, Midas, and Goodyear. Meineke charged less than the others, with a median price of $150, versus $170 for Car-X and Goodyear, and $180 for Midas. Firestone and Sears satisfied significantly fewer customers than the other chains. Compared with other chains, Sears Auto Centers fared poorly. It exerted more sales pressure than others. More often than other chains, Sears didn't do the job right the first time, didn't have the car ready on time, used what our readers considered deceptive prices in advertising, and gave inaccurate estimates.

RATINGS: BRAKE SHOPS

Notes on the table Judgments reflect subscribers' experiences with repairs made between 1991 and 1993, based on 22,000 responses to *Consumer Reports* 1993 Annual Questionnaire.

Satisfaction summarizes readers' opinions about each shop. A score of 60 means the average reader was fairly well satisfied; 80, very satisfied; and 100, completely satisfied. For chains, a difference of four points or more in overall satisfaction is meaningful.

Within types, listed in order of general satisfaction

Shop	Overall satisfaction	Median price	
	0 20 40 60 80 100		
Independent garages		$150	
New-car dealers		200	
REPAIR CHAINS			
Car-X		170	
Meineke		150	
Midas		180	
Goodyear Auto Service		170	
Firestone (Mastercare Service Centers)		180	
Sears Auto Centers		200	

What to watch for

- Brake pads don't necessarily need to be replaced just because they squeak. Unless they're badly worn, the squeaking can often be cured by cleaning out dust, installing clips, or lubricating the backs of the pads.
- Some garages try to boost profits and save themselves time by installing new brake discs instead of smoothing the old ones on a lathe. Question the shop closely to see if you really need new discs or drums, particularly if your car is fairly new and the brake discs haven't been turned before.
- Be suspicious if the shop recommends a laundry list of new parts before service people have made a thorough inspection.

Better ◄——————————► Worse

Price is the median readers paid for repairs not covered by warranty. Factors that most influenced satisfaction included: **No problem** within a month after repair (70 to 90 percent of the time); little or **no pressure** for unneeded repairs (78 to 96 percent of the time); having the car ready **on time** (74 to 94 percent of the time). Judgments reflect readers' experiences and may not represent those of customers in general.

No problem	No pressure	On time	Location	Comments
◑	⦿	◑	Local	—
◑	◑	○	Local	Dealers do lion's share of work under warranty; service under warranty generally less satisfactory for our readers.
○	○	◑	Midwestern states	—
○	○	◑	All states except Ark., Hawaii, Kan., Ky., Mont., N.D., S.D.	—
○	○	○	Nationwide	—
○	○	○	Nationwide	—
○	○	◒	Nationwide	—
●	◒	●	Nationwide	Estimates less accurate than average.

MUFFLERS

For mufflers, as for brakes, *Consumer Reports* readers found that independent garages did more satisfactory work than franchised chains or new-car dealers.

Independent repair shops were more likely than chains to fix the muffler right the first time and to do the work without pressuring the customer for additional repairs. But one chain, Cole Muffler, matched the independents in customer satisfaction, and some others came close. Prices were also fairly comparable. The independents charged $120 for muffler work on average, while the chains charged $125. New-car dealers, on the other hand, averaged $180.

RATINGS: MUFFLER SHOPS

Notes on the table Judgments reflect subscribers' experiences with repairs made between 1991 and 1993, based on more than 12,000 responses to *Consumer Reports* 1993 Annual Questionnaire.

Satisfaction summarizes readers' opinions about each shop or type of shop. A score of 60 means the average reader was fairly well satisfied; 80, very satisfied; and 100, completely satisfied. For chains, a difference of five points or more in satisfaction scores is meaningful.

Price is the median readers paid for repairs not covered by warranty.

Within types, listed in order of general satisfaction

Shop	Overall satisfaction	Median price	Accurate estimate	On time
Independent garages		$120	O	O
New-car dealers		180	O	O
REPAIR CHAINS				
Cole Muffler		100	O	◓
Car-X		110	O	O
Midas		130	O	O
Meineke		120	O	O
Monro		120	O	O
Speedy Muffler King		125	O	O
Sears Auto Centers		110	◓	◓

Muffler chains may also offer an advantage over most independents: the convenience of while-you-wait service. According to the readers, 87 percent of muffler chains handled a repair in a few hours, compared with 55 percent of the independent garages and only 44 percent of new-car dealers.

The highest-ranked muffler chains are both regional: Cole in three states and Car-X in the Midwest and Florida. The two largest national chains, Midas and Meineke, ranked slightly lower in customer satisfaction but were still quite good overall. People who took their cars to Sears Auto Centers were the least satisfied overall. Compared with the top-rated chains, Sears turned in more than its share of prob-

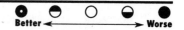

Better ◄—————————► Worse

Receiving an **accurate estimate** and having the car ready **on time** were among the factors that most affected satisfaction. Shops completed repairs on time 85 to 100 percent of the time; they gave an accurate estimate 93 to 99 percent of the time.

Except as noted in the Comments, the chains were not significantly different from each other in other factors, such as fixing the car right on the first attempt and inflicting undue sales pressure. Results reflect readers' experiences and may not represent those of customers in general.

Location	Comments
Local	Often failed to give written estimates.
Local	Often failed to give written estimates.
N.Y., Pa., Fla.	Good at fixing car right the first time; little sales pressure.
Midwestern states, Fla.	—
Nationwide	—
All states except Ark., Hawaii, Kan., Ky., Mont., N.D., S.D.	—
Conn., Mass., Md., N.H,. N.J., N.Y., Ohio, Pa., Vt., Va., W.Va.	—
Eastern states	—
Nationwide	More sales pressure than at some other chains.

lems with undue sales pressure, repairs done incorrectly, and repairs that were completed late.

What to watch for
- If part of the exhaust system fails, the mechanic may also want to replace most of the rest of the system, even though other components are still sound. That may seem excessive—but generally, it's not. It usually makes no sense to add one new component at a time; the parts of the exhaust system are often welded together or rust together, so they're hard to separate without damage.
- Watch out, however, if a mechanic wants to replace the catalytic converter simply because it's "rusty." A converter quickly acquires a veneer of rust, but there's no reason to replace it unless it leaks or stops working. You can expect the catalytic converter to last 100,000 miles or more.
- The U.S. Environmental Protection Agency requires automakers to guarantee converters for the car's first 50,000 miles. As of 1995, that will increase to 80,000 miles.
- When you have a car's exhaust system repaired, be especially careful to check the wording of the warranty. Some warranties cover only one specific part of the exhaust system, such as the muffler, but not the attached parts. If that's the case, having a second muffler job performed under warranty can wind up costing nearly as much as the first job did.

TRANSMISSIONS

Transmission repairs are the automotive equivalent of a root canal. Transmissions, particularly automatics, are complex devices that can be costly and time-consuming to fix. You often can't tell whether you need a minor adjustment or a major overhaul, so you're at the mercy of a mechanic who has every incentive to recommend major surgery. On the whole, our readers were far less satisfied with transmission work than with brake or muffler repairs.

Some 6,000 readers responded concerning their experiences with transmission work. That was enough to let *Consumer Reports* single out AAMCO, the largest transmission-repair chain (half of all readers who went to a chain went there), and to draw some general conclusions about car dealers, chains, and independent repair shops.

Nearly 60 percent of the survey respondents took their transmission troubles to a car dealer's service department, largely because they thought the repair would be covered by warranty. Around 30 percent went to an independent garage, and 10 percent went to a chain. Readers who went to an independent garage were most satisfied, followed by those who went to car dealers, then those who went to AAMCO or other chains. AAMCO wasn't significantly different from other chains in overall satisfaction.

Repair costs tended to increase as cars accumulated mileage. For cars with more than 60,000 miles, the median repair cost was $800 at chains, $500 at independent garages and dealers. AAMCO charged more than other chains for such cars—$820 versus $700.

Transmission repairs typically required more than two days —and often took longer than the mechanic had promised. About 30 percent of people who went to chains and new-car dealers, and 20 percent of those who went to independent garages, said they had to wait more than a day longer than they expected to get the car fixed.

Often, too, the transmission didn't stay fixed. About a fifth of the people who went to a dealer or an independent garage, and a third of those who went to a chain, had a further problem with the transmission a month after the initial repair. The great majority went back to the same shop to fix the problem. While two-thirds of the garage customers who had problems with the initial repair ultimately came away satisfied, more than half of the chain and car-dealer customers said they still weren't happy with the result.

About four out of five readers who used a chain received a warranty for the repairs, while fewer than half who went to local garages or dealers had a warranty. But only 56 percent of the readers using a chain were happy with the way the warranty was honored.

What to watch for

- For transmission work, it's especially critical to go to a mechanic you know you can trust—preferably one who has done good transmission repairs for someone you know. The average person simply has no way to tell whether a transmission problem is major or minor.
- Most readers who used a local garage either went to a shop they had used before or one that had been recommended to them.
- If the car is drivable, be wary of dire warnings and a

TRANSMISSION REPAIR BY THE NUMBERS

Even though *Consumer Reports* didn't receive enough responses to rate individual muffler chains, it was able to compare all chains with garages and new-car dealers. Here's how they stack up:

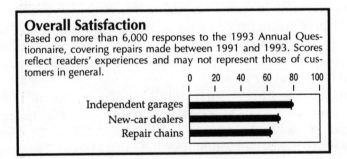

Overall Satisfaction
Based on more than 6,000 responses to the 1993 Annual Questionnaire, covering repairs made between 1991 and 1993. Scores reflect readers' experiences and may not represent those of customers in general.

Independent garages
New-car dealers
Repair chains

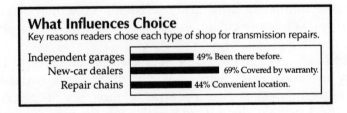

What Influences Choice
Key reasons readers chose each type of shop for transmission repairs.

Independent garages   49% Been there before.
New-car dealers   69% Covered by warranty.
Repair chains   44% Convenient location.

hard sell telling you that you must get a new transmission right away. Get a second opinion.

- Of the readers who went to a chain, about one in five said they felt pressured to have more work done. Garages and new-car dealers exerted much less pressure.
- Some shops will drop the transmission pan, point to any residue there, and cite it as proof that you need a new transmission. But a little residue is normal, particularly in an older transmission, and may mean nothing at all.

Pressure for Extra Work
Percent of respondents who said they felt pressured to have additional work performed.

Independent garages	5%
New-car dealers	8%
Repair chains	21%

Is Once Enough?
Percent of respondents who said they still had problems with the transmission within a month of the repairs.

Independent garages	20%
New-car dealers	23%
Repair chains	32%

Problems Linger On
Percent of respondents who had a problem with the initial repair and said they were dissatisfied with the way the shop remedied the problem.

Independent garages	34%
New-car dealers	58%
Repair chains	59%

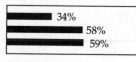

Appendix: Addresses and Phone Numbers

Send for the free *Consumer's Resource Handbook* for addresses and phone numbers of additional state and local consumer protection agencies; state insurance regulators; the national customer relations departments of major automobile, auto repair, oil, tire, and insurance companies; and Better Business Bureau offices. Write to: Handbook, Consumer Information Center, Pueblo, CO 81009. Further information on auto insurance companies is in *Best's Insurance Reports: Property-Casualty*, available at many libraries.

Agencies Enforcing Auto Repair Laws/Regulations

ALASKA: Office of the Attorney General complaint intake handled by Better Business Bureau, 2805 Bering St. #2, Anchorage, AK 99503, 907-562-0704. **CALIFORNIA:** Bureau of Automotive Repair, 400 R St., Sacramento, CA 95814, 800-952-5210, 916-445-1254. **COLORADO:** Consumer Protection Unit, Office of Attorney General, 1525 Sherman St., 5th Floor, Denver, CO 80203, 800-332-2071, 303-866-5189. **CONNECTICUT:** Dealers and Repairers Division, Department of Motor Vehicles, 60 State St., Wethersfield, CT 06109, 203-566-2433. **DISTRICT OF COLUMBIA:** Dept. of Consumer and Regulatory Affairs, 614 H St. N.W., Room 108, Washington, DC 20001, 202-727-7080.

FLORIDA: Department of Agriculture and Consumer Services, Division of Consumer Services, 227 N. Bronough St., Suite 7200, Tallahassee, FL 32301, 800-435-7352, 904-488-2221; **Broward County:** Consumer Affairs Division, Broward County, 115 S. Andrews Ave., Room A-460, Ft. Lauderdale, FL 33301, 305-765-5355; **Dade County:** Consumer Services Department, Motor Vehicle Repair Section, 111 NW First St., Miami, FL 33128, 305-375-4222, Ext. 209, fax 305-375-3512. **HAWAII:** Department of Commerce and Consumer Affairs, Regulated Industries Complaints Office, P.O. Box 2399, Honolulu, HI 96804, 808-587-3222; prior complaint history: 808-586-2677. **IDAHO:** Office of the Attorney General, Consumer Protection Division, 700 W. Jefferson St., Room 119, Boise, ID 83720-0010, 800-432-3545, 208-334-2424. **ILLINOIS: Chicago:** Department of Consumer Services, City Hall, Room 808, 121 North LaSalle St., Chicago, IL 60602, 312-744-9400. **INDIANA:** Consumer Protection Division, Office of Attorney General, 219 State House, Indianapolis, IN 46204, 800-382-5516, 317-232-6330. **IOWA:** Consumer Protection Division, Office of Attorney General, 1300 East Walnut St., 2nd Floor, Des Moines, IA 50319, 515-281-5926. **LOUISIANA:** (New-car dealers only) Louisiana Motor Vehicle Commission, 234 Loyola Ave., Suite 1014, New Orleans, LA 70112, 504-568-5282. **MAINE:** Department of the Attorney General, Consumer Mediation Service, State House Station 6, Augusta, ME 04337, 207-626-8849. **MARYLAND:** Consumer Protection Division, Office of the Attorney General, 200 St. Paul Place, Baltimore, MD 21202-2022, 410-528-8662. **Montgomery County:** Office of Consumer Affairs, 100 Maryland Ave., Rockville, MD 20850, 301-217-7373; **Prince George's County:** Office of Citizen and Consumer Affairs, County Administration Bldg., Room L15, Upper Marlboro, MD 20772-3050, 301-952-4700. **MASSACHUSETTS:** (Body shops) Division of Standards, Executive Office of Consumer Affairs, One Ashburton Place, Room 1115, Boston, MA 02108, 617-727-3480, fax 617-727-5705; (Auto repair) Consumer Complaint Section, Office of the Attorney General, 131 Tremont St., Boston, MA 02111, 617-727-8400. **MICHIGAN:** Bureau of Automotive Regulation, Department of State, Lansing, MI 48918, 800-292-4204, 313-357-5108 (Wayne, Oakland, and Macomb). **MINNESOTA:** Consumer Division, Office of Attorney General,

445 Minnesota St., St. Paul, MN 55101-2131, 800-657-3787, 612-296-2331; **Minneapolis:** Licenses and Consumer Services Division, Operations and Regulatory Services, 350 South 5th St., Room 1-C, Minneapolis, MN 55415-1391, 612-673-2080. **MONTANA:** Department of Commerce, Office of Consumer Affairs, 1424 9th Ave., P.O. Box 200501, Helena, MT 59620-0501, 406-444-4311. **NEVADA:** (Auto repair) Consumer Affairs Division, Complaint Desk, Department of Business and Industry, 1850 E. Sahara Ave., Suite 101, Las Vegas, NV 89158, 702-486-7354; (Body shops) Dept. of Motor Vehicles and Public Safety, Registration Division, Bureau of Enforcement, 2701 E. Sahara Ave., Las Vegas, NV 89104, 702-486-4222. **NEW HAMPSHIRE:** Consumer Protection and Antitrust Division, Attorney General's Office, 33 Capitol St., Concord, NH 03301, 603-271-3641. **NEW JERSEY:** (Body shops) Motor Vehicle Services, Auto Body Licensing Unit, CN 172, 225 E. State St., Trenton, NJ 08666, 609-984-9633; (Auto repair) Division of Consumer Affairs, 124 Halsey St., Newark, NJ 07102, 201-504-6200. **NEW YORK:** Department of Motor Vehicles, Division of Vehicle Safety, Box 2700-ESP, Albany, NY 12228, 518-474-8943. **OHIO:** Office of Attorney General, Consumer Protection Division, State Office Tower, 25th Floor, 30 East Broad St., Columbus, OH 43215, 800-282-0515, 614-466-4986. **OREGON:** (Body shops) Insurance Division, Consumer Services and Enforcement, 440-2 Labor and Industries Bldg., Salem, OR 97310, 503-378-4018, Ext. 600. **PENNSYLVANIA:** Bureau of Consumer Protection, Office of Attorney General, Strawberry Square, 14th Floor, Harrisburg, PA 17120, 800-441-2555, 717-787-9707. **RHODE ISLAND:** (Body shops) Department of Business Regulation, Auto Wrecking and Salvage, 233 Richmond St., Providence, RI 02903, 401-277-2416. **TENNESSEE:** Division of Consumer Affairs, 500 James Robertson Parkway, 5th Floor, Nashville, TN 37243-0600, 800-342-8385, 615-741-4737, fax 615-532-4994. **TEXAS: Dallas:** Consumer Protection, Division of Building Inspection, Dept. of Economic Development, 320 East Jefferson, Room 118, Dallas, TX 75203, 214-948-4400. **UTAH:** (Repairs) Department of Commerce, Division of Consumer Protection, P.O. Box 45804, Salt Lake City, UT 84145-0804, 801-530-6601; (Body shop licenses/ surety bonds) Motor Vehicle Enforcement Division, Utah State

Tax Commission, 210 N. 1950 West, Salt Lake City, UT 84134, 801-297-2600. **VIRGINIA:** Dept. of Agriculture and Consumer Services, Division of Consumer Affairs, Room 101, Washington Bldg., 1100 Bank St., P.O. Box 1163, Richmond, VA 23219, 800-552-9963, 804-786-2042. **WASHINGTON:** Consumer Protection Division, Office of the Attorney General, 900 Fourth Ave., Suite 2000, Seattle, WA 98164, 800-551-4636, 206-464-6684. **WISCONSIN:** Division of Trade and Consumer Protection, Dept. of Agriculture, Trade and Consumer Protection, P.O. Box 8911, Madison, WI 53708-8911, 800-422-7128, 608-266-2225.

Federal Agencies

FEDERAL TRADE COMMISSION: 6th & Pennsylvania Ave., N.W., Washington, DC 20580; **NATIONAL HIGHWAY TRAFFIC SAFETY ADMINISTRATION (NHTSA):** (Recalls) auto safety hotline, 800-424-9393 or 202-366-0123 [TYY: 800-424-9153 or 202-366-7800]; (Service bulletins) Technical Reference Division, 400 Seventh St., S.W., Room 5110, Washington, DC 20590, 202-366-2768.

New-Car Warranty Arbitration

AUTOMOTIVE CONSUMER ACTION PROGRAM (AUTOCAP): National Automobile Dealers Association, 8400 Westpark Dr., McLean, VA 22102, 800-252-6232, 703-821-7144; **BETTER BUSINESS BUREAU AUTOLINE:** 800-955-5100; **CHRYSLER CUSTOMER ARBITRATION BOARD:** For address of regional board, call 800-992-1997 or write Chrysler Customer Center, P.O. Box 302, Center Line, MI 48015-9302; **FORD DISPUTE SETTLEMENT BOARD:** P.O. Box 5120, Southfield, MI 48086.

Automotive Organizations

AUTOMOBILE PROTECTION ASSOCIATION: 292 St. Joseph Blvd. W., Montreal, Quebec H2V 2N7, Canada, 514-272-

5555; Toronto office: 160 Pears Ave., Suite 322, Toronto, Ont. M5R 1T2, Canada, 416-964-6774; **CERTIFIED AUTOMOTIVE PARTS ASSOCIATION (CAPA):** 1518 K St. N.W., Suite 306, Washington, DC 20005; 202-737-2212, fax 202-737-2214; **CENTER FOR AUTO SAFETY:** 2001 S. St. N.W., Suite 410, Washington, DC 20009, 202-328-7700; **MOTOR VOTERS:** 1500 W. El Camino Ave., Suite 419, Sacramento, CA 95833, 916-920-5464, fax 916-920-5465.

Notes

1 Link v. Mercedes-Benz of North America, Inc., 788 F.2d 918 (3rd Cir. 1986).
2 Barnes v. Jones Chevrolet Co., Inc., 358 S.E.2d 156 (S.C.App. 1987).
3 Treadwell Ford, Inc. v. Campbell, 485 So.2d 312 (Ala. 1986).
4 Ayer v. Ford Motor Co. See *Antitrust and Trade Regulation Report* (The Bureau of National Affairs), September 16, 1993, p. 367; Max Gates, "Makers Can't Blame Lack of Parts to Dodge Lemon Law, Court Rules," *Automotive News*, July 12, 1993, p. 17.
5 Helen Kahn, "Calif. Judge Lashes BMW, Orders Big Lemon Payment," *Automotive News*, February 24, 1992, p. 23.
6 Helen Kahn, "Mercedes-Benz Loses N.J. Lemon Law Case," *Automotive News*, November 9, 1992, p. 41.
7 Paces Ferry Dodge, Inc. v. Thomas, 331 S.E.2d 4 (Ga.App. 1985).
8 State v. Pike, 826 P.2d 152 (Wash. 1992).
9 Rodio v. Smith, 587 A.2d 621 (N.J. 1991).
10 Ramirez v. Autosport, 400 A.2d 1345 (N.J. 1982).
11 City National Bank of Charleston v. Wells, 384 S.E.2d 374 (W.Va. 1989).
12 Joseph v. Hendrix, 536 So.2d 448 (La.App.1 Cir. 1988).
13 Young v. Century Lincoln-Mercury, Inc., 422 S.E.2d 103 (S.C. 1992) and Young v. Century Lincoln-Mercury, Inc., 306 S.E.2d 105 (S.C.App. 1989).
14 Melody Home Manufacturing Co. v. Barnes, 741 S.W.2d 349 (Tex. 1987).
15 AAMCO Transmission v. Air Systems, Inc., 459 N.E.2d 1215 (Ind. App. 2 Dist. 1984).
16 Berning v. Drumwright, 832 P.2d 1138 (Idaho App. 1992).

17 Huffmaster v. Robinson 534 A.2d 435 (N.J.Super.L. 1986).

18 Design & Funding, Inc. v. Betz Garage, Inc., 438 A.2d 1316 (Md. 1981).

19 Kopischke v. First Continental Corp., 187 Mont.471, 610 P.2d 668 (1980) and Crothers By Crothers v. Cohen, 384 N.W.2d 562 (Minn.App. 1986).

20 Dale v. King Lincoln-Mercury, Inc., 676 P2d. 744 (Kan. 1984).

21 Ismael v. Goodman Toyota, 417 S.E.2d 290 (N.C.App. 1992).

22 Warner v. Reagan Buick, Inc., 17 UCC Rep.Serv.2d (240 Neb.668) (Neb. 1992).

23 Morris v. Mack's Used Cars, 824 S.W.2d 538 (Tenn. 1992).

24 Peabody v. P.J.'s Auto Village, Inc., 569 A.2d 460 (Vt. 1989).

25 Roberts v. American Warranty Corp., Del.Super., 514 A.2d 1132 (Del. 1986).

26 Oettinger v. Lakeview Motors, Inc., 675 F. Supp. 1488 (E.D.Va. 1988).

27 Williams v. Toyota of Jefferson, Inc., 655 F. Supp. 1081 (E.D.La. 1987).

28 Berrie v. Toyota Motor Sales, USA, Inc. See Steven P. Bann, "Breach of Warranty Not Required to Prove Automobile Is a Lemon," *New Jersey Law Journal*, October 4, 1993, p. 41.

29 Williams v. Chrysler Corp. 530 So.2d 1214 (La.App. 2 Cir. 1988) and 532 So.2d 133 (La. 1988).

30 Henderson v. Chrysler Corp. See *Michigan Lawyers Weekly*, October 21, 1991, p. 8.

31 Ramirez v. Autosport, 400 A.2d 1345 (N.J. 1982).

32 Andrews v. Scott Pontiac Cadillac GMC, 594 N.E.2d 1127 (Ohio App.6 Dist. 1991).

33 Volkswagen of America, Inc. v. Dillard, 579 So.2d 1301 (Ala. 1991).

34 Jeep Eagle Sales v. Mack Massey Motors, 814 S.W.2d 167 (Tex.App., El Paso 1991).

35 Mercedes-Benz of North America v. Dickenson, 720 S.W.2d 844 (Tex.App., Fort Worth 1986).

36 Pirozzi v. Penske Olds-Cadillac-GMC, 605 A.2d 373 (Pa.Super. 1992).

Index